the new york book of wine

By Matthew DeBord

universe publishing

First published in the United States of America in 2003
by UNIVERSE PUBLISHING
A Division of Rizzoli International Publications, Inc.
300 Park Avenue South
New York, NY 10010
www.rizzoliusa.com

2003 2004 2005 2006 2007/ 10 9 8 7 6 5 4 3 2 1

Distributed to the U.S. trade by St. Martin's Press, New York

Printed in the United States of America

ISBN: 0-7893-0997-1

Library of Congress Catalog Control Number: 2003104946

contents

preface

New York is a big city. A very big city. Full of places to buy,
drink, taste, and trade wine. In fact, of all the cities in the
world, New York probably offers to the wine consumer—
whether rank amateur or seasoned expert—the most daunting
array of wine choices anywhere on planet Earth. Yes, yes, Paris
is also full of wine—but it's mostly French wine. Rome is no
slouch either. But in New York, wine is truly a global experience.

But where to begin this international journey in wine?
This book will provide you with a bevy of suggestions, from
wine bars to restaurants and wine stores to the wineries themselves (New York state has plenty). Along the way, I'll dispense
tips to keep you savvy as your wine knowledge and experience grows.

If you're a beginner, you'll probably want to start with a
"Brief Primer on Wine," which offers a crash course in types
of wine and related terminology. But if you're already confident with your basic knowledge, then use the book as a guide
to the best that New York has to offer.

Please remember: Wine is just a beverage. Sure, it's a
beverage rich in cultural and historical associations. But at the
end of the day, you can still wash down your hamburger with
Château Haut-Brion and think of it as nothing more than a
pleasant pairing. The decision to go snobby is yours and
yours alone. I advise against it.

In the end, you owe it to yourself to take advantage of all
the incredible wine that this restless, constantly-craving-
something-fresh-and-new city invariably attracts. You might
get briefly frustrated, even confused, or bewildered. But
you'll never regret the effort.

introduction

a new york frame of wine

Welcome to New York. Now go find a place to have a drink. Yes, New York has never suffered from a lack of beery watering holes. But the city has always taken its wine pretty seriously, too. You can live many different lives in the Big Apple—and sophisticated connoisseur of the finer things is certainly one of them.

How to sort it all out? When you get right down to it, the trick is dedication. New York rewards the intrepid explorer's mentality, so the first step to mastering the city's many wine options is to strap on a pair of sturdy shoes and start walking around. Wine stores don't charge admission, and the most you'll pay for a glass of wine at a wine bar is . . . well, you can pay a lot for a glass of wine at a wine bar these days (we're talking the realm of the $25 pinot noir by the glass here).

But don't let that discourage you, because it's a *good* thing. A few years back, even though the wine business in America was booming, wine bars were still something that people returning from Europe were talking about. However, New York has lately seen an explosion of these establishments, which come in very handy for trying out new wine styles and trying expensive labels you'd otherwise be reluctant to sample—or might not even be able to *obtain*. Even better, many have become genuine nightspots and fairly good restaurants in their own rights (less intimidating than full-scale restaurants, but nonetheless employing talented chefs and knowledgeable staffers). They're also terrific places to spend time if you're single and past the 25¢-beer happy-hour scene.

Wine bars are, in other words, an excellent place to begin your journey through New York wine. Restaurants are another.

It's hard to exaggerate just how important the city's restaurants are to the wine scene. It's here that celebrity chefs and hot-shot sommeliers combine their skills to kick off wine-drinking trends. Don't believe me? Ask yourself how seriously New Yorkers took Italian wines before Mario Batali—or for that matter French wines before André Soltner and the original Lutèce. A few years ago, New York's restaurant wine pros could almost single-handedly claim credit for starting a mini craze in Austrian wines, some of the world's most obscure (up to that point, anyway). But they knew that Gothamites would take to them. New Yorkers have never shied away from risk, especially when it comes to eating and drinking.

The majority of New York restaurants that maintain an educated wine program also offer an ever-changing lineup of wines by the glass, so you're never going to be stuck in a situation where you have no choice but to buy a $50 bottle of chardonnay. (Not that you shouldn't: Wines by the bottle are almost always a better deal than wines by the glass, and I'll explain why later in the book.)

Eventually, of course, you'll graduate from ordering and drinking your wine out and start thinking about enjoying your wine at home. In which case it will be time to get serious about wine shops—not that the liquor store on the corner where you've been buying Chilean jug wines for the past few years isn't a serious establishment. But when it comes to buying wine in New York, the key—as with just about everything else in this city of sharp judgments and endlessly reinvented personalities—is to know who the real players are. There are about two dozen wine stores in Manhattan that define the scene, and the sooner you get acquainted with them, their specific selections, and their very professional staffs, the better your New York life in wine will be.

In the beginning, however, it can all be pretty confusing. So many labels, so little time. A wine course is a good idea.

First of all, you'll meet similarly enthusiastic people with whom you can develop informal wine friendships. But you'll also learn the difference between Old World and New World wines, about wine-making techniques, the importance of vintages, and in the end acquire a host of other skills you need to be a better wine consumer.

Finally, armed with an abundance of knowledge and a wealth of experience, you're going to want to see some grapevines firsthand. Maybe you've already traveled to the wine regions of Europe or California and think New York has nothing similar to offer. Wrong! New York is literally crammed with vines, as close to the New York metropolitan area as Long Island, and as far away as the picturesque Finger Lakes region, five hours north of the city by car (and thus not a bad candidate for a wine-tour getaway weekend).

Your indispensable tool in all this is going to be curiosity. You have to be prepared to see New York as a wine town par excellence, as the best wine city the world has ever known! Does that sound like overstatement? Well, maybe. But then, this is New York. Understatement doesn't fly here, in wine or anything else. So welcome to *The New York Book of Wine*. It's ambitious. It's a little gruff sometimes, even pushy. But it knows what it's talking about. Read on, New York wine lover. Read on.

Chapter One

a brief primer

wine in new york

from colonial grog to prohibition and beyond

New York, founded in 1625, has always been a drinking town. It was called New Amsterdam by its original Dutch masters and the inhabitants then enjoyed a drink as much as they do now (although they probably drank rum, not wine). During colonial times, the quaff of choice was Madeira, a nearly indestructible wine, imported from an island off the coast of Spain, that could survive the long sea voyage from Europe to the New World. Thomas Jefferson famously and unsuccessfully struggled to introduce wine-grape cultivation to his native Virginia, horrified that the new American nation was becoming a country of beer and spirit swillers. He should have focused more effort on New York, where European wines were already highly regarded among the upper crust.

In the nineteenth century, the imbibing habits of Gothamites progressed as the new nation developed into an international trading power. From the period after the Civil War, through the Belle Époque and into the early twentieth century, things really took off. New Yorkers began to get rich, and just as they sought cosmopolitan validation from European capitals such as London and Paris, they began to mimic the drinking customs of Old Worlders. French and German wines were all the rage. At restaurants, you could buy first-growth bordeaux by the quart (these were the days before the neighborhood wine shop).

New Yorkers continued to enjoy their unique position in the wine world right on through the teens, until Prohibition was enacted. In addition to destroying the burgeoning American wine industry—which was, as you might imagine,

centered on New York state—Prohibition sent drinking in
New York underground. Famous speakeasies, such as the legendary '21' Club, catered to a clientele that was willing to
break the law for a sip of wine.

Or, more commonly, liquor. After Prohibition's repeal,
New York became better known as a cocktail-and-beer town.
Wine drinking, while present, was viewed as a preoccupation
of elite gourmets—who had been to Europe and seen what
they considered to be true wine culture in action—and immi-
grants, who at one time had been part of those cultures the
gourmets so admired and hoped to emulate.

It took decades for the American wine industry to
recover. California, by virtue of its superior climate for growing premium wine grapes, took the lead. New York,
meanwhile, revived its relationship with European wines. In
the fifties and sixties, wine connoisseurship in New York
meant drinking French wines, often at French restaurants. It
required a new generation of restaurateurs to interest the Big
Apple in the wines of the Golden State.

Eventually, of course, they succeeded too well. For a
while in the eighties and nineties, California wines—especially
chardonnay and merlots—seriously displaced wines from
France, Italy, Spain, and Germany.

Over time, however, the Old World and New slipped into
a New York sort of détente, as innovative Italian restaurateurs
began to promote the fine-wine revolution in Italy. New
Yorkers rediscovered the wines of France, especially robust
Rhône reds and the internationalized varietal of Languedoc.
Bordeaux staged a revival with its stunning 2000 vintage, and
restaurants and wine stores dedicated themselves wholly to
the esoteric wines of Burgundy.

South American–themed restaurants showcased Argen-
tine and Chilean wines, and even Riesling, a long-neglected
but superb variety that reached its pinnacle in Germany, came

roaring back, as the "anything but chardonnay" reactionaries gained sway.

Now, in the early years of the twenty-first century, the wine scene in New York is more dynamic than at any time in its history. Smart retailers have opened wine shops that make it easy to find and buy wines. Wine bars are popping up all over town. Even the little neighborhood mom-and-pop restaurant feels obliged to offer diners something more than the house red and the house white. Wine courses are popular. The *New York Times* recently ramped up its wine coverage. "Wine is a necessity of life for me," Thomas Jefferson once remarked. No one has taken that sentiment to heart more than the city of New York.

a rundown of wine varieties

Here's how it works: By and large, New World wines (California, Australia, Chile) are typically identified by grape variety: chardonnay, merlot, cabernet sauvignon. Old World wines are identified by producer or appellation: Château Haut-Brion, Côtes du Rhône, Mersault. There are exceptions—Riesling seems to be Riesling just about everywhere—but basically New Worlders focus on grapes while Old Worlders fixate on where the grapes came from or who made them into wine. Obviously, the New World way is simpler, and it has begun to be adopted in the Old World, but it's also less colorful.

✣ Whites

Grape type: Chardonnay
Main regions of production: Burgundy, Australia, California
Flavor profile: You name it—crisp and steely to plush and

fruity to creamy and oaky. A main grape variety in champagne and many sparkling wines. Perhaps the most popular grape in the world.

Grape type: Sauvignon blanc
Main regions of production: France, California, New Zealand
Flavor profile: Citrusy, with herbal and mineral notes in France; fruity and sometimes grassy in California; aggressively citrusy in New Zealand, sometimes showing an exotic, tropical flavor the locals refer to as "gooseberry." Can even exude a unique, difficult-to-place aroma colloquially known as—get this—"cat pee."

Grape type: Riesling
Main regions of production: Germany, France, Australia, New York state
Flavor profile: Ranges from off-dry to rather sweet. Germany shows the greatest breadth, incorporating everything from lemons and limes to coconuts and apricots. Similar styles are being produced in New York's Finger Lakes regions, about a five-hour drive north of New York City.

Grape type: Gewürztraminer
Main regions of production: Germany, France, New York state
Flavor profile: Riesling's slightly floozier cousin. Aroma is intensely floral, flavors are fruity and often spicy. Best examples hail from Alsace, but versions can be found around the world.

Grape type: Viognier
Main regions of production: France, California
Flavor profile: France's Rhône produces Condrieu, richly floral with tropical flavors and full body; in California, it's fruity but less complex. An unusual wine that has a sort of cult following, especially among the "Anything But Chardonnay"

crowd, a loose coalition of wine lovers who have had it with chardonnay's ubiquitous exposure.

Grape type: Pinot Grigio/Pinot Gris

Main regions of production: Italy, France, Oregon

Flavor profile: America loves pinot grigio! After chardonnay, this simple Italian wine is the country's most popular white. Flavors are straightforward: citrusy, with body that varies depending on wine-making style. In France and Oregon, pinot gris, as the grape is called outside Italy, can be vinified in a dry or off-dry manner, producing somewhat more brooding wines that can reveal aromas of smoke and flavors that include complex mineral aspects.

❊ Reds

Grape type: Cabernet Sauvignon

Main regions of production: France, California (especially the Napa Valley), South America, Australia

Flavor profile: Diverse, depending on where grown. Rich, dark red fruits—blueberries and blackberries—cassis, kirsch, bell pepper, olives, herbs, eucalyptus, mint, chocolate. Cabs that have been stored in oak barrels can show vanilla and toast notes. Older cabs and cab-based wines can develop "brown," mature flavors that suggest tobacco, cedar, cigar boxes, and leather to some tasters. The very best, older cabernets, mainly from Bordeaux, often become extremely smooth and enticingly aromatic. The king of grape varieties.

Grape type: Merlot

Main regions of production: France, California, New York state, South America, Australia

Flavor profile: Produces softer, plusher, and fruitier wines than cabernet. Flavors include dark red fruits, such as dark cherries, blueberries, and plums. Chocolate sometimes appears in Californian and Chilean versions.

Grape type: Pinot noir
Main regions of production: France, California, Australia, New Zealand, Oregon
Flavor profile: In France, pinot noir produces the great reds of Burgundy, whose flavors can range from light raspberry and cherry to almost chocolatey, depending on vintage. New World versions tend to be juicier and fruitier, but without as much acidity or structure; they are accordingly considered to be less able to age. Older Burgundies exhibit exotic aromas and flavors, running a gamut from wet earth to, believe it or not, manure. Many tasters detect "mineral" (i.e., rocks and stones, particularly chalk and slate) flavors in French red Burgundies and attribute these to the vineyard sites where the grapes were grown. An important component in some champagne and sparkling wines.

Grape type: Cabernet Franc
Main regions of production: France, New York state, California
Flavor profile: Lighter and more florally aromatic then cabernet sauvignon. Tasters often detect cherry, raspberry, violet, and chocolate flavors.

Grape type: Malbec
Main regions of production: France, Argentina
Flavor profile: Very powerful and tannic wines, but usually rather rustic. Traditionally, a blending grape in Bordeaux. In Argentina, more refined, fruity wines have been produced from the Malbec grape. Best French examples are from the southern region of Cahors.

Grape type: Sangiovese

Main regions of production: Italy, California

Flavor profile: Sangiovese is the main component of the famous wines of Chianti, but also of the legendary Brunellos of Tuscany. It also features in what are known as Super Tuscan wines, which are reds made in a more international style, often with cabernet sauvignon and merlot blended in. Sangiovese itself is an acquired taste: It is not typically a powerful, fruity wine. Instead, its flavors tend to be firm and light, reminiscent of red fruits. There is often a bitter aspect, as well, which Italians enjoy, but some international drinkers find off-putting. A Sangiovese variation, Sangiovese Grosso, makes up Brunello di Montalcino, Tuscany's longest-lived wine.

Grape type: Nebbiolo

Main region of production: Italy

Flavor profile: Nebbiolo is an exotic grape that is something like the pinot noir of Italy. In its youth, the wines made from it can be almost undrinkable, extremely firm and mouth-puckeringly acidic. Give them a few decades, after which they evolve into velvety, seductive wines layered with complex aromas and flavors. The best examples, in their maturity, have the arresting ability to smell and taste almost exactly like the white truffles that have made the grape's home region, Piedmont, a mecca for gourmands.

Grape type: Syrah/Shiraz

Main regions of production: France, Australia, California

Flavor profile: Syrah is the most important grape in the powerful, dense, fiery wines of the northern Rhône in France. In Australia, where it's known as Shiraz, it's smoother and fruitier, characterized by its pepperiness. It gives us the country's greatest wine, Penfolds Grange. In Santa Barbara, California, winemakers are making terrific wines from Syrah.

Grape type: Zinfandel

Main Region of Production: California

Flavor profile: This is the great American grape, long cultivated in California. When you hear a zin referred to as Old Vine, you should imagine something special: grapes that were spawned from massive, gnarled, mature vines that have been around forever. Zins are typically rich, robust, highly alcoholic wines, bursting with fruit flavor, sometimes thick with an under layer of dark chocolate. Once you get addicted to them, it's hard to break the zin habit.

Grape type: Petite Sirah

Main region of production: California

Flavor profile: If a big old zinfandel seems a tad twee for your tastes, then maybe Petite Sirah is where your heart lies. Wines made from this grape have a savage, primitive quality and often seem almost black in color. Drink a couple of glasses and you might have to brush your teeth three times before bed—it's been known to stain stainless steel.

Grape type: Gamay

Main region of production: Beaujolais, France

Flavor profile: Gamay is the grape that gives the world Beaujolais Nouveau, the most popular exported French wine in . . . well, the history of French wine exports. (You know when it's Nouveau time in New York [November] because the wine stores put up their "Beaujolais Nouveau est arrivé!" signs.) Gamay also goes into Beaujolais' so-called "cru" wines, which are of much higher caliber than the soda pop–like Nouveau, but not so pricey that they don't represent a great undiscovered bargain in French wine.

reading more about it

At times, it seems as if there are more wine texts than wine drinkers. There are, however, a few you can't live without. But before you hit the books, you might want to check out one of the wine periodicals. The finest of these is the large-format *Wine Spectator*, which combines comprehensive coverage of all the world's major wine regions, along with extensive tasting notes, travel features, restaurant coverage, profiles, and other wine-culture journalism. Hardcore oenophiles sometimes scoff at *Spectator*'s glossy extras, preferring to get their info from Robert M. Parker, Jr.'s newsletter, *The Wine Advocate*, which consists almost entirely of tasting notes. There is another newsletter also worth checking out, Stephen Tanzer's *International Wine Cellar*. (And everybody has some kind of Internet presence nowadays.) Other glossies worth considering are the frisky *Wine & Spirits*, the stately (and British) *Decanter*, as well as *Food & Wine* and *Gourmet*, both of which are pitched more at food lovers, but contain plenty of wine information in each issue (don't miss plucky wine editor Lettie Teague's frequent tales of wine adventure in *Food & Wine*). Where books are concerned, you should focus on five: Oz Clarke's *New Wine Atlas*, Jancis Robinson's *The Oxford Companion to Wine*, Andrea Immer's *Great Wine Made Simple*, Kermit Lynch's *Adventures on the Wine Route*, and Jay McInerney's *Bacchus & Me*.

starting out: wine bars

wine bars

Wine bars are a relatively new development in New York. They've been all the rage in Paris and especially London for a while now, but they've only just begun to catch on in Manhattan. This is because New Yorkers have traditionally liked to do their drinking—their real drinking, as opposed to drinking with meals—in bars. They have also tended to favor one of two beverages: beer or cocktails. It's well known—and copiously documented, by everyone from Joseph Mitchell to Pete Hamill—that New York, when not fueled by good old-fashioned ales and lagers at places like McSorley's, has run on cocktails whipped up by expert mixologists at swank venues, such as the Stork Club and the Rainbow Room.

However, with the advent of the wine boom in the 1990s, plenty of New Yorkers—including those who had grown tired of the Kandy-Kolored Kocktail Kraze (see: Cosmopolitan)—decided that it might be fun to drink wine socially, while out on the town, instead of only at home and in restaurants.

The entrepreneurial sorts behind the new wine bars responded intelligently, by hiring chefs (or at least cooks) to provide sippers with a steady supply of small nibbly foods. Some restaurants simply expanded their space to include a wine bar and designed a special menu to serve there.

Now, it seems as if there's a new wine bar opening every week. In fact, some wine bars have become so popular, and apparently profitable, that they now seem almost like restaurants in their own rights.

Several have even become white-hot nightspots, singles clubs with good wines, pick-up joints with vintage listings. Or at least a nice place to go for a first date and to split a bottle.

Keep in mind, when visiting a wine bar, that you are already in defiance of my by-the-glass warning, which dictates that when you drink wine by the glass, you are almost always getting ripped off. At wine bars, however, the markups tend to be slightly lower than at regular restaurants, simply because every wine served at a wine bar tends to be by the glass. Still, you are better off drinking by the bottle. But, it's worth pointing out, the whole idea behind a wine bar is to sample several different wines in one sitting. And remember, in most cases, you won't be spending as much on food. Unless, of course, you order a dozen small plates. It can all add up fast.

the bubble lounge

✳ *228 W. Broadway*
212-431-3433
$$$

Like champagne? You're not alone, as this somewhat cooled (but once very hot) watering hole in Tribeca will show you. This is where people even better-looking than those you might find at Punch & Judy (see page 26) go to get their bubbly fix. And it is truly a lounge, with lots of comfy seating, both upstairs, where the lighting is better, and downstairs, where the lighting is candlelit low, and kept that way on purpose. It can be a bit of a hassle to gain admission, particularly on a weekend, when the velvet rope has been known to come out. But once inside, you can confidently part with much cash as you sample some of the 25 champers available by the glass or delve into the nearly 300 bubblies offered by the bottle. Didn't know there were 300 kinds of champagne in existence? Boy, do you need the Bubble Lounge, and bad.

The absolute can't fail wine to order

Champagne. Yes, that's right, bubbly. Forget white, forget red, forget rosé. Order something with fizz. Well, only if you're completely stumped, stymied, or otherwise perplexed. Why champagne? Mainly because it's almost always good. Sparkling wines may sometimes disappoint, but champagne rarely does. For one thing, most types of champagne don't depend on the vagaries and caprices of vintage; they are instead blended from various years, to achieve a consistent level of quality and a reliable house "style." Krug is always supposed to taste like Krug. Taittinger is always supposed to taste like Taittinger. And so on. There are fluctuations, and certain premium champers are released in vintage years. But for the most part, champagne is your safest bet in an increasingly diverse and confusing wine world. It's like buying stock in IBM: totally blue chip. Champagne is generally blended from chardonnay, pinot noir, and occasionally a third grape, pinot munier. The wine has to be blended because the region of its production is located in just about the most marginal growing area in all of France. If you drank any of the wines that go into champagne before their secondary fermentation in the bottles (the cause of the fizz), you'd probably never drink champagne again. These "component wines" need to undergo changes before they're ready to be set free as the most famous wine on Earth. This they do, to delightful effect, so much so that even obscure, small-producer champagne are wonderful. And wonderful with a far wider range of foods than you might think. In fact, you can easily match champagne with just about everything except grilled beef.

Soups, stews, game, pasta—the sky's the limit. Champagne is also a terrific choice for drinking all the way through lunch. When it comes to matching wine with food, champagne is the bulletproof choice.

i trulli

�֍ *122 E. 27th St.*
212-481-7372
$$$

I Trulli's wine bar is adjacent to the restaurant. It's a lovely, relaxing place to sample one of the many Italian wines on the rather large list. You can also order pretty much anything you want off the restaurant's menu, so there's no reason not to think of this wine bar as one that performs double duty as a dinner spot. Of course, the real way to play it is to meet up here, share a glass or two of sparkling Prosecco, then move on to heavier lifting. One thing you can be sure of, given that I Trulli's owners operate a wine store across the street, is that every Barolo and Brunello you try will have been stored under ideal conditions and handled with care. This is not a state of affairs that you can assume at stand-alone wine bars that don't have a similar stake in moving bottles retail.

le bateau ivre

✖ *230 E. 51st St.*
212-583-0579
$$

This wine bar is as French as they come, right down to the name, taken from a poem by Gallic versifier Arthur Rimbaud. It's also one of the earliest attempts at a wine bar in New York. The location isn't great: smack in the middle of Midtown east, not exactly a neighborhood renowned for nursing the hip and trendy. Its lineup of wines is also quite extensive, a departure from the newer practice, seen at places such as Punch & Judy, of keeping it tight. In short, it's a wine bar based more on the French model, where the idea is to offer customers plenty of choices. The menu supplies basic bistro fare, and there's a decent amount of outdoor seating. Evenings in June, Le Bateau Ivre does take on a vibe straight out of the Marais, with professionals dropping in to converse or carouse.

What to watch or listen to when you drink

Some serious wine geeks will tell you that wine is best tasted under nearly Proustian conditions, in a window-less soundproof room with nothing extraneous on hand to distract from the demanding business of evaluating your vintages. I think this notion is ridiculous. Why in the world wouldn't you combine your pleasures? Wine is, after all, one of the best aids to relaxation that humanity has yet devised, so what could possibly be wrong with slipping a beloved CD into the stereo—or calling up a trendy tune on the MP3 player—or, heck, emulating an old fogey like myself and slapping a hunk of vinyl on the turntable when it comes time to savor some wine? When I was working at *Wine Spectator*, we polled readers on their wine-and-music preferences and discovered that they match wine with styles of music with the same opinionated enthusiasm (maybe more) than they bring to the challenge of matching wine with food.

michael jordan's wine bar

❋ *Grand Central Terminal, 23 Vanderbilt Ave.*

212-655-2300

$$$

Never thought we'd see MJ and wine bar in the same sentence. Michael Jordan's Steakhouse makes sense. But His Airness is also a wine lover, so it was natural that the Glazier Group, which manages the already very popular steakhouse, would want to extend the brand, as it were, into the burgeoning wine-bar scene. Of course, their decision was made easier by the fact that the space now occupied by the wine bar used to be a sort of gift shop dedicated to all things Mike, and made a strange entrance to the restaurant itself, which is distinguished by an entrancing view of Grand Central's main concourse. Nobody seemed to want to buy a Number 23 jersey to go with their steak. Enter Scott Carney, a wine pro who designed a savvy by-the-glass list and collaborated with the chef to develop a bar menu. Mike's wine bar isn't large, but it is gracious, and the wines it features are typically wonderful, drawn from the restaurant's cellar. Unlike other wine bars in Manhattan, there really isn't a proper bar here, with a guy standing behind it, doling out pours of Syrah. Instead, there is a long, high, barlike table in the middle of the room, with wine-storage cases off to one side. Customers are attended by regular waitstaff. It's different, but don't knock it until you've tried it.

morrell wine bar & cafe

❋ *1 Rockefeller Plaza*

212-262-7700

$$$

Punch & Judy might be the hippest wine bar in New York (see page 26), but Morrell is the best. The brainchild of Nikos

Antonakeas, Morrell & Co.'s auction director, this lively, elegantly appointed space stocks plenty of wines by the glass, with everything available for purchase right next door at the wine shop. Now, you might think that such close proximity to a tourist trap like Rockefeller Center would cause problems, but it most assuredly doesn't. Stepping into Morrell Wine Bar is a lot like taking a quick flight to Paris—you feel instantly insulated from hoi polloi. A lot of this is due to obsessive attention to detail: Frette linens, perfect bread in the bread basket, the wonderful cuisine of chef Michael Haimowitz, the carefully chosen list of 100 (yes, 100) wines by the glass. The selection is dazzling. California pinot noirs, outstanding French Burgundies, rare Australian reds, even more rare French dessert wines, such as the coveted Sauterne Château d'Yquem (tough to find by the glass). Plenty of folks come to Morrell expecting to have one drink and leave having had half a dozen, plus a bottle, plus dinner. The beautiful two-level space, with bottles displayed in glass cabinets and French posters decorating the walls, doesn't want to let you leave. The management understands this allure; they recently opened a second location downtown.

punch & judy

❊ *26 Clinton St.*

212-982-1116

$$

Surely the coolest wine bar on the entire planet. Who knew? Certainly not the management. They just wanted to open a groovy place where Lower East Side hipsters could go to enjoy something other than Rolling Rock or Brazilian cocktails. But the place took off, and now it's packed practically every night, with foxy chicks and slick dudes. Lately, even a slumming uptown grownup or two can be found here, drinking Grenache or the latest groovy offering from Ribero del Duero, or possibly an Australian Riesling. The owners, Constantine Mouzakitis and Giacomo Turone, deserve their success: They have created a luxuriously casual, candlelit space—all dark wood, exposed brick and intimate tables—then added Riedel stemware and a lineup of beckoningly trendy wines. They hit it out of the park when they hired Dominick Guiliano to be their chef; the man, who works in a tiny space not much bigger than the backseat of an old Checker cab, is responsible for the city's best wine-bar fare. It's no challenge at all to make a meal of his creations (the carpaccio "sushi" roll, is pure genius). You might think it would be difficult to spot Punch & Judy from the street, because, in keeping with the Lower East Side ethic, there's no sign. They don't need a sign; just follow the stream of attractive people on the hunt for wine.

dining and wining out

All right, it's time to get serious. Of course, anybody who visits or lives in New York spends some time in restaurants. New Yorkers take dining out as seriously as some other cultures take religious worship.

In the past ten years, the wine scene at Gotham's many, many eateries—both posh and relatively quotidian—has been significantly altered. Frankly, wine in the Big Apple's restaurants used to be so intimidating it was easy: Most establishments that maintained decent lists stocked them with impressive French wines—Bordeaux classified growths, coveted Burgundies, champagne—and paid little attention to the rest of the world. These were mainly French restaurants anyway, so there was no reason to consider the non-French wine world.

Everybody else, particularly the Italian restaurants, tended to maintain small, rather woeful lists that emphasized inexpensive quaffers—cheap reds, cheap whites—and included maybe half a dozen high-caliber bottlings for the big spenders. The house wine, whatever that was, worked for most folks.

Everything changed in the eighties and nineties. Wine suddenly became a far more important aspect of the New York dining landscape. Just as chefs at restaurants that had nothing to do with haute cuisine became stars, sommeliers—formerly thought of as waiters who wore suits and knew how to properly decant the few older wines that were sold each year—achieved the cultural status of dining-room wine gurus.

Wine lists also evolved. They got global. In the early days of New York restaurants (we're talking the 1890s here, by the way), most wine lists featured French and German wines almost exclusively. It wasn't until the 1960s and seventies that California wines even popped onto the radar screens of most restaurateurs.

Gradually, more and more wine lists—and more and more of the carefully assembled, compact lists that began to define smaller restaurants—started to feature California bottlings. Then Australian. Then South American. By the late nineties, it was possible to dine out at dozens of places in Manhattan and see no French wines whatsoever on the lists.

There has been a bit of an adjustment in recent years, especially as numerous neo-bistros and neo-brasseries have proliferated, bringing along with them lists heavily canted toward French wines. California wines, as a result of the nineties wine boom, have also become more expensive. In some cases, ironically, California wines are pricier than the French wines that they once sought to displace, and are now being displaced by—ah, what comes around goes around!

Nowadays, you almost need a degree in international relations to sort out even the shortest list. But, as you might imagine, I have some tips for you.

how to read a wine list

❋ Step one: Scan

You're looking for something you've had before, either at another restaurant or at home. You want to see how it's priced. The general rule at New York restaurants is to price the wine at two-to-three times retail. So a merlot that cost you $15 in a store will cost you at least $30 in a restaurant. Get used to this markup, odious as it may seem. Maintaining a decent wine list—not to mention staying in business as a restaurant in the country's most ferociously competitive market—is a real financial challenge. Many restaurateurs use the wine markup to sustain their yearly profits. The wine press periodically complains about this, but they don't have much of a case. Yes, it would be great if wine were cheaper at restaurants. But then it would probably be cheap wine.

Besides, if you're dining out at a place that takes wine seriously, why would you be obsessed with price?

That said, there is a threshold you do not want to cross. In my book, there's not much point in spending more than $75 on wine at a restaurant in New York (unless it's a special occasion and you've set your sights on something hard to find that a restaurant happens to have). Some people say you shouldn't spend more than $50 or $60. I think you need to be more flexible than that. Anywhere else, sure, keep it under $60. But in New York, that extra $15 can get you into some phenomenal stuff that's actually a bargain—given that as wines on lists rise in quality and wholesale price, the markup often declines (restaurants want to move these wines, after all).

❈ Step two:
Don't buy the cheapest wine on the list

Everyone knows this tenet (who wants to look cheap?). Ironically, restaurateurs are well aware of the tendency and will sometimes move a slow-selling cheap wine to the second- or third-cheapest category as a psychological tactic. Once you've scanned the list and figured out the relative markup, you can decide between the cheapest wine and the ones that go for $75.

❈ Step three:
When stumped, choose a region or varietal and focus on vintage

This is where expertise on vintage comes in handy. For example, just about everything from Tuscany in the 1997 vintage is going to be pretty good. Likewise 1994 in Northern California. You might also want to be aware of so-called "restaurant vintages." Why? Well, let's say you know that 1995 Brunello di Montalcinos are superb and considered impressive by wine writers. Ditto 1997 cabernets. What are the chances that those wines will be drinkable before 2005 at the earliest? Not good. More solvent and ethical restaurateurs and wine professionals will hold back these longer-lived vintages. Others will price them high and try to capitalize on good press. You are too smart for this. You know that 1996 and 1997 were not great vintages in Bordeaux, but the wines are perfectly drinkable now and furthermore, higher in acidity and thus good with food. They'll probably be priced to move, as well.

✽ Step four:
Ask for the sommelier's help

These people live and breathe wine and love to share their knowledge and passion with others. Well, most of the time they do. Sometimes they're just trying to get rid of some stock. The best way to deal with them is to explain what you're going to be eating (everyone in your party) in order to give them a sense of what you like. Then let them run with the information. Most of the time, they'll steer you right. However, be careful about appealing to waitstaff, in the absence of an on-the-floor sommelier. Sometimes regular waiters have received wine training, sometimes they haven't. At less snazzy restaurants, they will have in all likelihood been given a briefing on the day's wines by the glass at the very least. But they still might not know what they're talking about.

✽ Step five:
If the sommelier is clearly an amateur or trying to sell me something I think is too expensive, what should I do?

Wing it. If there's nothing on the list you know, and the sommelier is determined to sell you that $100 bottle of chardonnay, choose the second-cheapest German or Alsatian white. There have been no truly horrible German or Alsatian vintages in a decade. You can't miss. If there are no German or Alsatian wines on the list, stick to wines $30 or below from Australia or New Zealand—these wines are crowd-pleasers and will almost certainly not disappoint.

❖ Step six:
Should I sniff the cork?

Under no circumstances. If you buy a glass of wine, the server should bring you a nice, clean stem that's appropriate to the wine you've selected, and he or she should show you the bottle, so you can confirm that you're getting what you ordered. If you buy a bottle, the server or sommelier must show it to you, indicating producer, style of wine, and vintage ("Mondavi, Cabernet Sauvignon Reserve, 1997"). If the cork doesn't come out cleanly, make the server take the wine back and open a fresh bottle. (The exception would be an old bottle, whose cork might have degraded, but to no ill effect on the wine. This wine will have to decanted, but we'll get to that in a second.) If the cork is crisply popped, the server will place it on the table, for you to inspect. This is so that you can study the cork and confirm that it matches the bottle you ordered. There was a time—a more corrupt time—when shady winemakers would try to fake famous wines, so the famous producers began to use the cork as a form of confirmation, imprinting it with the name of their estate and sealing it in a foil capsule.

❖ Step seven:
Who tastes the wine?

Whoever ordered it. You have to get used to taking charge if you're going to drink wine in restaurants. The server or sommelier will pour you a small taste. Give it a swirl, sniff it to determine whether it's corked or otherwise flawed, then taste it. If there's something obviously wrong, ask the server or sommelier to taste and get their opinion. If the wine seems fine, nod or say, "Okay" or "Good," then observe as the server pours everyone else a few ounces, never filling the glasses all the way up. You can't properly swirl, sniff, or appreciate a full glass of wine.

✳ Step eight:
The server keeps coming around and topping off the glasses. I'd rather do this myself. What's the call?

Tell the server that you want to pour the wine yourself. It's not hard to suspect that they're topping off everybody so diligently because they're trying to get you to buy a second bottle. Maybe. But sometimes they're just enthusiastic. However, it's your bottle of wine, you paid for it. And you certainly wouldn't allow the waiter to cut your food, would you?

wine matching challenges

Okay, you've got wine. But what if you discover that you're drinking a big, gutsy zinfandel and there's nothing on the menu but fish? You might want to first ask yourself why a fish joint would have a big, gutsy zin on the list to begin with. But the real issue is: How do you match wine with food?

Whole books have been written on this topic and entire careers dedicated to the question. Cracking cold fusion is nothing to these people. Because, by God, they're going to figure out a way to drink wine with artichokes.

The truth is, the old rules about drinking reds with beef and game and whites with chicken and fish have pretty much been tossed out the window. Crisp, fruity pinot noirs, for instance, go very well with sweet, oily salmon. Riesling can easily wash down bison steaks. Cabernet sauvignon is nice with roast chicken.

There are a few danger areas, however. Here are a few:

Vinegar: There's a reason why Europeans like their salad at the end of the meal. Vinegar, which in some cases had its start as wine, doesn't often get along with wine. Lots of appetizers can involve vinegar or vinegary items (pickled items, for example, and condiments like ketchup). Keep your eyes peeled.

Artichokes: Amusing to eat, but they also tend to make wines taste sweet. Best to serve them at the beginning of a meal and match them with crisp white wines.

Asparagus: This one has never bothered me, but it does some. I've found that zingy, acidic whites are best, if you must. Sauces, such as the classic hollandaise, can offset the problem.

Asian and Indian cuisines: The endless challenge. Mexican and South American, with all the fat and meat mixed in with wine-unfriendly hot peppers and spice, is easier. But because Asian cuisines so often mix spicy and sweet flavors and use difficult-to-match ingredients such as ginger in copious amounts, most wine pros recommend sticking with off-dry, semisweet or sweet wines, like Riesling. This can work just fine. In fact, I think it's the only thing that works. Asian food plays havoc with most other wines—understandable since Asian cuisines did not emerge from same intense wine cultures as, say, France or Italy. Indian is the same, but slightly less tricky. You can get away with the somewhat richer reds. Strangely, American food—and by this I mean things like hamburgers and meatloaf—is more wine-friendly. Just lay off the ketchup. And as far as Asian and Indian goes, hey, these are New York takeout staples. There's no harm in periodically taking a break from wine and drinking beer.

the best restaurants for wine drinking

Although almost every restaurant in New York has some kind of wine selection, each of the restaurants I've listed here maintains what I would define as serious wine programs. Their wine lists generally try to cover as much of the world of wine as possible or if they do focus on only one country, their list will be exhaustive. They will not only include bottles that only oenophiles would recognize—and collect—but wines that will delight everyone.

alfama

551 Hudson St.

212-645-2500

$$

Alfama falls into a category of restaurants that New York always needed but didn't have: a place that specializes in the cuisine and wines of Portugal. Real lovers of European wine know that Portugal is justifiably famous for its port, a type of fortified wine. But they also know that Portugal sustains a large still-wine industry—and that the wines, particularly the reds, are some of the best values going (some might even know that the best-selling Mateus Rosé, the lightly fizzy wine so well-known to tyro drinkers in the 1970s, hails from Portugal). Portuguese cooking is also something of a revelation; in the eyes of many, it's superior to Spanish. There's a rustic purity to it that its slightly more highfalutin Iberian neighbor lacks. Better yet, it's a natural with wine. A word to the wary: Portugal isn't like the rest of the world. The country's winemakers haven't yanked out all their obscure native grape varieties to make room for cabernet sauvignon and merlot. Consequently, Portuguese wines can run a gamut from gruff to refined. And, given that even educated consumers can

have a tough time finding Portuguese wines in the market-place, you're pretty much in the hands of Alfama's skilled staff when it comes to wine selection. If you're feeling independent, however, the reds of the Dao are a good place to start, and some of the country's port houses, located in the Duoro region, are raising their profiles as still wine-producers.

artisanal

❊ *2 Park Ave. (enter on 32nd St.)*
212-725-8585
$$

Most New Yorkers think of this Terence Brennan–owned brasserie as the place that put the city onto its current obsession with cheese. To be sure, there's plenty of cheese to be had—either in its pure form, compliments of the stand-alone cheese counter, or in classic cheese-driven dishes, such as the various sinfully addictive fondues. But there's also a wine list, and, glass for glass, it's one of the most diverse in town. There's almost no way to order from it and be disappointed. In fact, this is the only New York restaurant where I routinely break my own by-the-glass rule and order two or three different selections over the course of a meal. It isn't cheap, but it sure is educational. I've enjoyed everything from Loire reds to southern French whites to Aussie fruit bombs. And I've never had anything to complain about. This is one wine list that covers a lot of ground. Naturally, they'll be able to suggest something that goes perfectly with whatever cheese—hard, runny, or stinky—that you might be considering.

aureole

❖ *34 E. 61st St.*

888-968-7836

$$$$

Chef Charlie Palmer's flagship is very important in New York's recent restaurant history. Palmer, who at one point traveled the world learning all he could about cooking, successfully joined uptown style with less uptight downtown culinary trends in this absolutely gorgeous Upper East Side space, a revamped townhouse. The food was fresh and simple—although very expertly executed—while the restaurant's décor was welcoming to diners who spent the bulk of their evenings at such stalwarts as Lutèce and La Caravelle. From the beginning, Palmer wanted to mirror what he had seen in Europe with his restaurant, fully merging fine wine with the overall dining experience. Arguably, he has succeeded better in this task with his Las Vegas outpost, where a wine "tower" is attended by "angels" who rise up and down on tethers, theatrically retrieving bottles. New York lacks that circuslike touch, but there's nothing wrong with Aureole's list. It's canted toward French wines, but Palmer has discovered California (he operates a new restaurant in Sonoma and has talked about someday moving there permanently), so expect that area of the list to grow.

az

❖ *21 W. 17th St.*

212-691-8888

$$

Oh, boy, this place had its work cut out for it when it came to wine. Chef Patricia Yeo's cuisine took New Yorkers by storm several years ago, with it daring synthesis of all the main fusion trends that were floating around at the time. The restaurant's dramatic design, which features a vast skylight that can be shaded depending on weather conditions, upped the ante. Now, I'll be the first to argue that fusion and wine is a tough match. This is because fusion, which generally draws much inspiration from Asian culinary ideas, includes plenty of ingredients that give wine fits. The trick is to develop a wine list that isn't going to be the kind of thing you'd spot at a steakhouse or a French bistro. You need something more eclectic—something far better curated—than that. AZ has pulled it off and hasn't been forced to resort to suggesting Riesling or Gewürztraminer with every dish in the process.

Drinking different wines during a meal

Why limit yourself to one wine per meal? I mean, maybe you don't feel like a middle-of-the-road cabernet Franc, which can pair with just about anything. If this is your mood, then I recommend sampling a wine by the glass with your first course, then moving on to a bottle of red with the main course, and perhaps finishing up with a glass of dessert wine or Port. Note: That white by-the-glass can easily be a glass of champagne or sparkling wine, and maybe should be. If you're me, it could also be a Martini.

babbo

❊ *110 Waverly Place*
212-777-0303
$$$

esca

❊ *402 W. 43rd St.*
212-564-7272
$$$

lupa

✳ *170 Thompson St.*
212-982-5089
$$$

These are the three jewels in the Bastianich/Batali restaurant empire (another, which isn't really a jewel yet, is pizza joint–cum–wine bar Otto). Babbo is the showpiece, housed in the former Coach House, just off Washington Square Park. It's here that Batali expanded the culinary ideas he had developed at his romantic, minuscule debut, Po, on Greenwich Village's mini Restaurant Row, Cornelia Street. Batali, who grew up in Seattle and worked early on as a pizza-maker, cut his Italian teeth in the Emilia-Romagna region, a somewhat obscure part of central Italy that features a cuisine rich in caprice and contradiction (sweet and spicy counterpoints are common). Babbo itself is currently the most famous Italian restaurant in town—a haunt of everyone from Tiger Woods to assorted movie stars to local jazz musicians, such as guitarist and crooner John Pizzarelli. The bar is always packed (it's a great place to squeeze in an introductory dinner, by the way). Both the upstairs and downstairs dining rooms are visions of elegance of comfort, staffed by waiters and waitresses who bring new meaning to the concept of casual confidence. Lupa, farther downtown, near the border between the Village and Soho, is Batali's interpretation of a Roman train-station trattoria. Everything here is more rustic, with a robust cuisine constructed in honor of Mario's favorite animal, the glorious pig. The restaurant is also about twice—no, make that five times—as noisy as the more stately and sedate Babbo. Esca is a complete departure from its two siblings, a fish place located dauntingly far west, just off the Theater District, a section of town considered by those in the know to be a culinary wasteland (for the most part). Esca's decor is far more minimal than Babbo's or Lupa's—one might even say cool, if not for the mellow lighting. The bar is a treat, because it's there that the day's catch is vividly displayed, on ice, in a circular display. Ice also lines the bar itself, so that the bartender can perch oysters on it, or just use it to chill your bottle of white wine. Signature dish? Crudo, or Italian sushi. And what about the wine? Well, the program is as serious as can be, without over-reaching. The lists at all three places are Italian, Italian, Italian, spanning all the country's considerable offerings. Sure, Babbo seems oriented more toward the high end—with its Barolos and Brunellos—while Esca carries more fish-friendly wines, including some newly trendy, lively whites from Friuli, a region in Italy's northeast corner. Lupa specializes in the savage reds of newly hip southern Italy but still keeps more than a few familiar Tuscan reds around. But basically the Bastianich/Batali wine holdings are of a piece. For my money, all three restaurants offer what has to be considered a boon to wine connoisseurs: an ever-changing by-the-glass service that isn't served by the glass. Rather, selections are presented in small decanter-size portions, variations on the Italian quartino, or quarter bottle. This enables diners to control their pour, which, given Babbo's, Lupa's, and Esca's investment in premium stemware, is a welcome thing.

barbetta

❄ *321 W. 46th St.*
212-246-9171
$$$

Over the past decade, New York has experienced an explosion of rustic Tuscan-themed trattorias that serve good, honest Italian chow that represents a slightly—and sometimes even significantly—higher standard for residents accustomed to the red-sauce joints of yesteryear. Unfortunately, in the rush to deliver authentic urban renderings of cooking based on olive oil and hearty pasta sauces—and raise it to the level of a modern-day haute cuisine—the style of dining that once defined high Italian has gotten lost.

In Italy, they often talk about "the butter belt" that separates the cuisine of the North, which uses butter, from the cuisine of the South, which uses olive oil. Barbetta is most decidedly north of the butter belt. It's even located in the wrong 'hood for proper modern-day Italian eating—the Theater District. The style of cooking here is Piemontese, meaning creamy sauces, delicate, delectable stuffed pastas, risotto, and meat as the main course. There's nary a tomato in sight—but there is plenty of sumptuous drapery, acres of white tablecloths, and an extremely dignified waitstaff (the dining room, with its preposterously aristocratic Old World mood, always reminds me of something out of the great Italian movie *The Leopard*). The wine list is equally Piemontese in orientation, full of terrific Barberas, Barolos, and Barbarescos—the Burgundies of Italy. Unlike the richer reds of Tuscany and the South, these wines have a crisper, more acidic profile. But they reward careful cellaring. Enter Barbetta's talented, spring-loaded sommelier, Leo Frokic, who knows his way around this somewhat esoteric realm. He can even clue you in on the very trendy whites of Italy's northeastern corner, which bear a far closer resemblance to German wines than anything the rest of Italy has to offer.

barolo

❖ *398 W. Broadway*
212-226-1102
$$$

For a period of time, in the early-to-mid 1990s, Barolo defined Soho dining style. This large, open restaurant, with its backyard garden and sidewalk seating in spring and summer, joined see-and-be-seen Soho munching and Old World Italian cooking, updated according to the tastes of the artsy set and their appreciation of a lighter cuisine. On the wine front, the list is appealing if not outstanding, with plenty of selections from northern Italy, as well as more crowd-pleasing entries from other parts of the country. There's something slightly Euro about the whole vibe, right down to the radical nineties notion that a nice dinner with wine is a viable alternative to a night of cocktails and barhopping.

bobby van's steakhouse

❊ *230 Park Ave.*

212-867-5490

$$$

People go to steakhouses for stupid reasons. Or maybe it's just that they don't commit before leaving the house. Bobby Van's, which has been around for a while and is currently experiencing a minor renaissance, demands some commitment. Just agree beforehand that you are (1) going to eat a nice piece of aged beef and (2) wash it down with a sturdy red wine. If you want fish, go to Le Bernardin. The wine program at Bobby Van's isn't nearly the equal of Sparks (see page 54) but the service is professional, and there's more than enough California cabernet—not necessarily the best steak wine but certainly America's favorite steak wine—to keep committed carnivores properly lubricated.

daniel

❊ *60 E. 65th St.*

212-288-0033

$$$$

Daniel is, by popular agreement, the best French restaurant

in New York—at least for the moment. The beautiful establishment, which so deftly blends an easygoing dining experience with a sense of classic French luxury, is also the only restaurant in town routinely lauded by *The Wine Advocate*'s Robert Parker (there was even a rumor several years ago that Parker had died here, after he had collapsed due to what turned out to be a non–life threatening ailment). The restaurant's sommelier—a slick dude named Jean-Luc LeDu, who favors chunky black spectacles and snappy ties—was immortalized for his hipster leanings by novelist and wine writer Jay McInerney. The restaurant's eponymous chef, Daniel Boulud, is regarded as Manhattan's most consistently brilliant professional. A dinner at Daniel is, in boom or bust times, the closest thing most New Yorkers can find to a sure bet. The food, of course, is generally phenomenal—classic French technique thoroughly modernized. The wine program is outstanding, both deep and broad, but with a natural emphasis on the mother country. First-growth Bordeaux abounds—not to mention luxury Cuvée champagne. It is not exactly affordable to the average wine consumer, but that's not really the point. With the exception of certain Upper East Side burghers, captains of media, and ladies who lunch, Daniel is a special-occasion destination.

felidia

❖ *243 E. 58th St.*

212-758-1479

$$$

Before there was Babbo, Joe Bastianich's mother, Lidia, had Felidia, where she served New Yorkers who were weaned on red-sauce joints in Little Italy the unusual cuisine of north-eastern Italy. It was kind of shocking when it opened, but like many initially shocking restaurants, it has mellowed nicely.

The mood here is dignified yet comfortable, a balance that visitors to Italy will be familiar with, but that diners accustomed to West Coast casual service will not. Another thing: The wine list is huge. Sommelier Richard Luftig oversees a cellar that contains nearly 50,000 bottles. The list itself features more than 1,000 selections. This is extravagant by Italian restaurant standards. The strengths are northern Italian wines, but you can find just about anything you may have heard of. As at the Bastianich's partnership restaurants with Mario Batali, a region to keep your eye on is Friuli, which produces Italy's best white wines.

guastavino's

❊ *409 E. 59th St.*

212-980-2455

$$$

Wow. Let me say that again: Wow. Tucked under the Queensboro Bridge on Manhattan's East Side, this might be the most visually spectacular restaurant in the entire city—compliments of Sir Terence Conran, the British design guru and restaurateur. It certainly feels as if it were conceived and built during boom times (it was). I'm not even sure a word like "vast" can adequately describe the place. It's transvast. Mondovast. Simply huge. Two levels of sprawling dining. The food is pretty good, but not as stunning—or intimidating—as one might expect. Basically, it's upscale comfort fare. The wine list—particularly the one at Club Guastavino, a cozier room separate from the main space—is smartly assembled, with a focus on more easygoing California wines.

l'acajou

❉ *53 W. 19th St.*

212-645-1706

$$

This cheerful, cozy bistro, located just west of the Flatiron District's dining hot zone, is deeply appreciated by a certain caliber of lunchtime customer, one seeking a respite from the rigors of a day at the office. Before Silicon Alley came along, L'Acajou was well-known among the publishing and advertising professionals who labor in this part of town for its welcoming bar, its snug, stylish room, and its devotion to such Parisian brasserie favorites as steak frites, tartes, omelets, and other satisfying, basic dishes. The wine list is another story. Not large, it stakes its claim to fame on its preoccupation with the wines of Alsace, a region in eastern France that sits on the German border. Every year, L'Acajou hosts an Alsatian wine festival, at which customers can experience the joys of a great Gewürztraminer, pinot gris, or Riesling. Of course, you don't have to wait—L'Acajou pours the glories of Alsace year-round. Pull up a stool at the bar, dig into a merguez sandwich, and open a copy of the *New York Post*. You won't feel like you're in France—but you will feel as if you'd like to be.

la caravelle

❉ *33 W. 55th St.*

212-586-4254

$$$$

In many respects, La Caravelle is the *echt*-dowager Midtown restaurant. This is where Jacqueline Kennedy Onassis liked to go for lunch. The main dining room is decidedly not what the contemporary New York diner claims to want, in this hypercasual day and age: starched white tablecloths, pink banquettes, colorful murals, and waiters who speak French.

The food, however, is au courant. A few years back, owners Rita and André Jammet decided to raise the old girl's temperature a few degrees. They imported Troy Dupuy, a classically trained chef from New Orleans, and let him loose. The result is some of the most fantastic cooking currently available in New York. Dupuy is slightly under the radar—he's not as well known as Daniel Boulud, Alain Ducasse, or Eric Ripert, but he should be. He has a way with old school French, updated and energized for modern tastes. He's especially talented with fish. As far as wine goes, the Jammets have made an effort to expand the program. Of particular interest is the selection of champagne, a La Caravelle beverage if ever there was one.

le bernardin

✣ *155 W. 51st St.*

212-489-1515

$$$$

New York's dining elite are always debating among themselves which French restaurant in the city is best. These days, it seems that Daniel rules the Gallic roost. However, Le Bernardin—due to the talents of chef Eric Ripert and dedication of Maguy LeCoze—holds a special place in the hearts of serious diners. I'll be the first to admit it: Right now, this nearly twenty-year-old establishment is, in my opinion, New York's best restaurant, period. What's odd about this is that Le Bernardin, since it opened in 1986, has focused exclusively on fish. And this is the fish place to end all fish places. Ripert has distilled and perfected a combination of elegant, but blisteringly flavorful, French saucing and an obsessive attentiveness to his base material. The snapper arrives in an austere presentation, and then is sauced in such a way that the flavors rise from the plate, then practically tremble on your tongue. They do things with spring vegetables here that ought to be declared state secrets. Ripert also has the ability to make fish an entrancing entrée for people who normally demand meat. Wine is predictably fish-friendly, but the list is also strong on Burgundy and Bordeaux—which, intriguingly, are sometimes required pairings with Ripert's mesmerizing cuisine.

le cirque 2000

✳ *New York Palace Hotel*
455 Madison Ave.
212-303-7788
$$$$

It is what it bills itself to be: a circus, for better or worse. Sirio Maccioni, the restaurant's owner, impresario, and all-around guiding force, relocated his already popular establishment—then known simply as Le Cirque—from Park Avenue to Madison Avenue and reopened in 2000 with a radical new design, all wild colors and dramatic interior effects. Patrons were initially stunned but eventually ratified all of Maccinoni's madcap ideas. Fortunately, neither the stupendous food nor the extensive wine list, overseen by wine director Ralph Hersom, suffered during the transition. Le Cirque always had a bit of French accent, so French wine naturally assumes pride of place on the list. However, Maccioni knows that his clientele doesn't include just francophiles. We're talking movie stars and sports heroes here, a group that tend to want their fine wine to come from California. Le Cirque 2000 does not lack for fantastic cabernets, nor for Italian wines, which makes perfect sense given the lineage of the restaurant's flamboyant owner.

le perigord

New Yorkers tend to think of this dignified Midtown East French restaurant as a haunt for UN diplomats and couples with net worths so high they're rarely discussed in public. Yes, the crowd can be a bit stodgy. However, over the past few years, owner/impresario Georges Briguet has made great strides in getting the establishment's food noticed. His most recent hire is Jacques Qualin, an extremely talented chef who has a marvelous way of updating classic dishes. His frog legs, for example, can remind you of just how delicious the amphibian's limbs can be. He also has a way with game and is himself an avid hunter. No one handles caribou better (he slow cooks it to counteract the meat's natural dryness). The wine list is not as extensive as at, say Le Cirque 2000, but it is well-appointed in important French regions, notably Burgundy.

les halles

❊ *411 Park Ave. South*

212-679-4111

$$

This is the restaurant that put New York culinary punk Anthony Bourdain on the map. Surrounded by neo-brasseries—Artisanal, Balthazar—it's the closest thing to the real deal in Gotham. Much of this had to do with the liberal smoking policy (before the citywide ban in 2003). You could smoke anywhere in Les Halles, any time you wanted (some nights the place seemed as if it might stay open until dawn, specifically to serve the needs of nocturnal chain-smoking francophiles). As a result, the nicotine dinge that new joints strive to emulate is, at Les Halles, thoroughly authentic. The food is no-nonsense: brasserie cuts of beef, compliments of the restaurant's very own butcher, frites, sausages—hearty fare that's good to wash down with a basic red, maybe something from southwestern France. It's not a restaurant at which I would be inclined to drop more than $30 on a bottle.

montrachet

❋ *239 W. Broadway*

212-219-2777

$$$

New York restaurant maven Drew Nieporent operates several eateries through his Myriad Group, but this is the one that started everything off. It was also one of the first restaurants to move into the now trendy Tribeca neighborhood, which two decades ago was a desolate enclave of loading docks and dying factories. Few restaurants have inspired such lasting loyalty. This allegiance has something to do with the cooking, which was once the provence of New York culinary bad boy David Bouley (he had an infamous falling out with Drew, which led to his departure from the scene, only to resurface later with his own namesake establishment). But, as you might imagine from the moniker, Montrachet was a trailblazer in putting the wines of Burgundy on New York's radar. This is thanks largely to the tireless efforts of wine director Daniel Johnnes, who has probably done more to popularize the wines of this cultish French region than anyone in America. The list here is huge: 1,800 wines and counting, with a total cellar stock of 30,000 bottles. It is indeed a Burgundophile's dream, with verticals from every important vineyard and producer. Of course, if you want to abjure the Burgs, Johnnes has you covered: Lately, he's delved into the relative bargain wines of France's two hottest regions, the Rhône and the large southern region called Languedoc.

olives at the w new york union square

❖ *201 Park Ave. South*

212-353-8345

$$$

You want big, bold Mediterranean flavors? Then drop by this ultra-hip restaurant and sample Boston import Todd English's over-the-top cuisine. English made his name with pizza, which here is a study in exuberance. Sometimes, however, English's food breaks with the Mediterranean custom of keeping everything you cook tuned to wine. Okay, more than sometimes. But that doesn't mean the wine list isn't impressive. It features lots of hearty, robust bottlings, with an emphasis on—as you might expect—California and Italy, with nods to France. In many respects, it's the perfect high-end pizza wine list. Just don't try to find a match for English's mascarpone polenta.

ouest

❖ *2315 Broadway*

212-580-8700

$$$

The Upper West Side is a neighborhood that many New Yorkers long to inhabit but wouldn't think to visit for a night of fine dining. Formerly it was well-known as the home of more Chinese takeout places per square mile than Chinatown, which is a 'hood that people at least venture into for a restaurant meal. The perception was that people with families live up there. They need restaurants that think of food as something you put in a plastic bag and give to a guy with a bicycle. Of course, there were some restaurants that involved tablecloths and wine, but they tended to be . . . how shall we say? Pitched at the budget diner? With the exception of a few dowager establishments south toward Midtown, drinking wine at an Upper West Side restaurant meant getting a free glass of plum wine with your mu shu pork, or a carafe of the house plonk with your oversauced pasta special. It was, in other words, a fine-dining wasteland. Restaurateurs tried and failed to rectify this. Enter Tom Valenti, and his confident, almost swaggeringly inviting bistro, Ouest (French for "west"). The wine list isn't, in the end, as ambitious as Valenti's plan to reinvent the Upper West Side's palate, but it does contain plenty of rich French reds to pair with the chef's version of hearty, stick-to-your-ribs Gallic fare.

river café

❖ *1 Water St. (Brooklyn Heights)*

718-522-5200

$$$

In my book, this is a great restaurant to take your parents to. Or your wife. Or your new girlfriend. Or your Uncle Louie from Canarsie. Heck, there's really no reason not to visit River Café (any excuse will do), which offers, from its perch on the edge of Brooklyn Heights, an absolutely stunning view of the Brooklyn Bridge, the East River, and Lower Manhattan. The food here is sturdy and sensible, nothing too exotic. The real star is the wine list, which has been tended for the better part of two decades by Joe Delissio, New York's most talented homegrown and self-taught sommelier. Delissio, a native New Yorker who, as they say, knew nothing from wine, was essentially raised at River Café. He started out low in the pecking order, but quickly discovered that he possessed both an affection for and an interest in good wine. So his bosses put him in charge. Now, he presides over a list of great breadth and intelligence, ranging from France and California to Australia. There's a little game you play with the River Café list, called "find the bargain." Delissio puts them in there on purpose (at least I think he does) and challenges fellow wine nuts to root them out. It takes time, but in its own charming way, reminds Delissio, I suspect, of where he came from and what got him to where he is.

sparks steakhouse

❊ *210 E. 46th St.*

212-687-4855

$$$

Red meat. Red wine. It's really that simple. Throughout New York, which is a truly great steakhouse town, carnivores debate the best place to go for grilled slabs of aged, marbled steer. We're talking about something so basic here—high-quality protein, an authentic vestige of the human species' hunt-for-your-dinner phase—that there's not much left to the imagination besides rampant opinioneering about who does it best. Peter Luger, a Brooklyn institution, usually gets the nod for New York's finest porterhouse. Others put in appearances: Smith & Wollensky, Bobby Van's, the Palm. But when it comes to matching wine with your steak, you gotta give the nod to Sparks. Sure, it's true that mob boss Paul Castellano met his bloody end here in 1985, and that the hit has secured Sparks a certain infamy. However, the joint is also justifiably famous for its spectacular wine cellar, which holds *Wine Spectator*'s prestigious Grand Award (one of only nine restaurants in Manhattan to merit the honor). The focus is on serious reds: California cabernets and Bordeaux. The atmosphere, which is masculine without suffering from the gruff, sawdust-on-the-floor vibe that characterizes other steakhouses, is perfect for red-wine consumption. My advice: Don't mess around too much. Get a nice cab and have your steak medium rare. You won't be disappointed.

Wines by the glass: useful, but generally a rip-off

It happens all the time. You sit down for dinner at a restaurant, can't find anything you can afford—or think you can afford—on the wine list, and resort to the wines-by-the-glass selection. Hey, a $10 glass of pinot noir certainly sounds better than a $40 bottle, right? Well, maybe not. Because if you do a little math, you'll discover that, in a standard-size wine bottle, there are about five "pours" or glasses of wine. Suddenly, your $40 bottle holds five $8 glasses. If you plan to have more than one glass of wine, you can make out better with the full bottle rather than the by-the-glass list. Of course, there are good reasons to take advantage of the by-the-glass list. You might be dining with people who all want something different, reds and whites, with their meals. Or you might only want a single glass, for whatever reason. And as by-the-glass lists generally offer a champagne or sparkling wine option, they can be a great way to start out a meal. Or end one, if there are dessert wines listed. However, restaurant wine pros know that they can make a better-than-average profit from by-the-glass lists. Restaurants usually mark up the bottles of wine on their list at least twice the retail value and sometimes three or even four times. Makes sense, if you think about it—especially when you consider that wines-by-glass lists have been known to feature glasses of wine priced at what you might pay retail for an entire bottle. Not a crime, just a point of understanding between seasoned diners and savvy sommeliers. And some use their by-the-glass lists to generously show-case difficult-to-obtain bottlings—California cult wines, for example—that they want to share with customers (hence the existence of wines by the glass that cost more than whole bottles). But there are other issues. Sometimes, wines by the glass are a bad bet because the restaurant or bar allows the opened bottle to sit out for far too long, causing the wine to oxidize and lose flavor. The best solution is to ask your server or sommelier to bring you the bottle, so you can examine the condition of the wine (and make sure you're getting what you ordered, especially if it's a rare and expensive wine). If you're worried about spoilage spoiling your meal, then stick with a bottle. It will, in all likelihood (assuming proper storage and handling) yield five glasses of better wine.

tribeca grill

❊ *375 Greenwich St.*

212-941-3900

$$$

In New York, it's not uncommon for a restaurant to open with great heralding and hoopla, complete with multiple celebrity sightings and great reviews, then close a few years later, once the buzz wears off. But this partnership between New York restaurant maven Drew Nieporent and actor Robert De Niro is still going strong, well into its third or even fourth act. So if a restaurant can survive its first brush with runaway fame, and if it combines the right elements, it can enter a happy middle age. That's just what's happened at Tribeca Grill, which now serves as an anchor for regulars and residents as well as repeat customers in its now-affluent neighborhood. The space itself is quintessential New York casual. A huge bar salvaged from the legendary Maxwell's Plum dominates the main dining room, which is decorated with art by De Niro's father. There's room upstairs for events and private dining, but most of the action is on the main floor. It's there that diners enjoy chef Don Pintabona's easygoing, classy comfort food. Pintabona's cooking is complimented by a wine list that's heavy on California bottlings, but hardly skimpy on other regions, such as Bordeaux, Burgundy, and especially the Rhône.

'21' club

❋ *21 W. 52nd St.*

212-582-7200

$$$

A lot of diners think of this former speakeasy, with its secret passageways and vaultlike, hidden wine cellar, as a theme park. Lunch here, at least for a while in the eighties and nineties, was a great chance to spot the city's movers and shakers fueling up on hamburgers and pot pies in the Bar Room, beneath a canopy of whimsical toys, donated by successful businessmen and sports heroes. You eased up to the stool-free (but not spittoon-free) bar, perched a foot on the brass rail, and ordered a martini. These remain appropriate ways to think about the most masculine restaurant in the city. But there have been some changes. For example, chef Erik Blauberg, in The Upstairs at '21'—a new space on the second floor, replete with fine linens and neoclassical murals—has departed from the classic menu that holds sway downstairs. Sommelier Christopher Shipley has also done some work on the wine list, which formerly was well-known for its devotion to blue-chip Bordeaux. There's a lot more California wine now, as well as Burgundy. Italy, the Rhône, and Spain are growing fast. There's even a plan to do more with—gasp!— white wine in the future. All 32 of the jockey statues that guard the restaurant's entrance rejoice.

union pacific

❊ *111 E. 22nd St.*

212-995-8500

$$$

Rocco DiSpirito, Union Pacific's owner/chef, is a lady-killer. Not to mention the star of his own reality-based television show, *The Restaurant*. The women of Manhattan can't get enough of this culinary innovator, whose good looks seem as if they might be more at home in a less sumptuous—borderline fantastical—restaurant (once you see the waterfall, you'll know what I'm talking about). But sumptuous it is—at least as far as restaurants in its trendy Flatiron/Gramercy Park environs go. DiSpirito, like many chefs of his generation, is preoccupied with Asian cooking, and it shows in his cuisine. The wine list here is also pretty enticing, even though it doesn't quite rise to the heights found at nearby Veritas. Not too hard, however, to find a versatile white to gracefully enhance both the food and an elegant second or even third date.

veritas

❊ *43 E. 20th St.*

212-353-3700

$$$

Veritas is generally regarded as having one of the top five wine lists in New York. In fact, the 2,000-plus label list is so good that some wags have maintained that the restaurant has reversed the usual organizing principle of the average eatery. Here, you have a gander at the wine list—which can be downloaded from the restaurant's Web site—before you look at the menu. (And, as you might imagine, some hardcore oenophiles research their selections in advance. You can even call ahead to have your wine decanted before you arrive.) Rules are flip-flopped: You match your food to your wine, not the other way around. The space itself is very nineties New York minimal and also fairly small. There's a decent-size (and often hopping) bar up front and a collection of tables in the snug, dimly lighted, and somewhat romantic dining room. Chef Scott Bryan has, understandably, customized his menu to match the bountiful selections on the vast wine list, which is housed in a fat, narrow binder. There really isn't a specialty. The list represents substantial portions of the personal cellars of the restaurant's partners and is accordingly eclectic—although thoroughly well stocked in virtually every major wine region. There's something for fans of Bordeaux, Burgundy, the Rhône, Germany, California, even Hungary! There are even some fine bargains to be had on older wines, if you know what you're looking for. In vino veritas? That's right.

enjoying wine at home

wine gear: where to buy what you need

There are any number of luxury retailers in New York who can supply you with exquisite crystal stemware: Fortunoff, Michael C. Fina, Bloomingdales. Unfortunately, the heavy, etched- or cut-crystal stems that used to be a staple of bridal registries have fallen decisively out of favor. Why? Because stemware needs to be about the wine, not the glass. A good general rule: Look for the simplest possible glasses you can find—but that still allow plenty of room for swirling, nosing, and studying your wine.

crate & barrel

❊ *650 Madison Ave.*
212-308-0011
611 Broadway
212-780-0004
www.crateandbarrel.com

As countless newlyweds have discovered, this national retailer with a big store in Midtown is not short of stemware. Fortunately, most of the designs are pretty serviceable. There are almost no offensive, overetched, or wildly colored examples to be had. Instead, there are generous balloons with thin rims and narrow stems, in a variety of shapes and sizes. I like the Nora 15-oz. red-wine glass: a simple, thin-rimmed tulip with ample space for nosing, which could easily be pressed into service as an all-purpose tasting and entertaining vessel. And at $8.50, the price is right. And, of course, as the registry of choice for New York's casual-chic brides, Crate & Barrel isn't short on anything else you might need to fully accessorize your wine-drinking life.

fishs eddy

✻ *889 Broadway*
212-420-9020

✻ *2176 Broadway*
212-873-8819

www.fishseddy.com

Nobody goes to Fishs Eddy to find delicate crystal stemware that will deliver an enlightening taste experience and allow connoisseurs to discern the subtle differences between a racy Sancerre and a voluptuous chardonnay. You go to Fishs Eddy to get cheap wineglasses that can survive the dishwasher. And Fishs Eddy isn't making any apologies for this state of affairs. Not at all, because this terrific store, which has several Manhattan locations, has always specialized in the sort of heavy, durable plates, glasses, and flatware that most Americans would recognize from roadside diners, coffee shops, and old-fashioned hotel restaurants. The stemware you'll find here is thick, chunky, and nearly indestructible. It's bad for tasting but ideal for large dinner parties (most people don't want to see their Riedels crash to the living room floor once party guests get a few drinks in them and start dancing). Several locations in Manhattan.

kmart

✻ *770 Broadway*
212-673-1540

✻ *250 West 34th St.*
212-760-1188

www.bluelight.com

New Yorkers were said to be horrified when this now-bankrupt (but still in business) discount retailer opened in the East Village. That was until the Martha Stewart merchandise showed up. The embattled tastemaker for middle America won over jaded Gothamites with her cheerfully retro designs.

KMart's stemware may not be the best, but Martha Stewart does offer some nice little juice glasses that are perfect for peasant-style Italian red-wine drinking. In case you're not up on Italian-peasant red-wine-quaffing customs, it's not exactly standard procedure—or wasn't, anyway, for a long time—to enter a quaint Italian trattoria and be greeted by colossal, and colossally expensive, wineglasses. Rather, you drink your simple *vino di tavola* from what amounts to an unadorned juice glass. It's fun, and a practice worth emulating every so often. Give the Balustrade line a shot. It'll do the job nicely and its etched band lends a pleasant Old World, *abondanza* feel to the set.

Wineglasses: The toughest easy decision you will ever make

In recent years, a dizzying number of wineglass styles have come onto the market. The finest of these, produced in Austria by George Riedel, profess to be able to maximize the olfactory and gustatory qualities of every style of wine available, not to mention a host of spirits. Riedels work, but they also cost more than other glasses, and they are rather fragile. If you get serious about tasting wine, it's nice to have one or two around, but for everyday drinking, a better choice might be a cheaper brand of stemware that can go into the dishwasher. I like the stems produced by a firm called Stoelze Oberglas, mainly because they mimic Riedels, but aren't so costly that I have a heart attack every time I break one. What you're after is a bowl of enough volume to allow for proper swirling and nosing of the wine. It should be tulip-shaped, with a thin rim, and the stem should be narrow rather than chunky so that the glass can be easily manipulated in the fingers. Everyone from Crate & Barrel to

Pottery Barn offers an acceptable version. But there is a single ironclad rule: no colored glass. Cut crystal should also be avoided. You want to be able to see your wine, uncolored and unrefracted.

pottery barn

❊ *1965 Broadway*
212-579-8477

❊ *600 Broadway*
212-219-2420

❊ *127 E. 59th Street*
917-369-0050

www.potterybarn.com

Crate & Barrel's slightly less glossy competitor (think earth tones and rough-hewn fabrics in place of minimalist white dinner plates) also offers a number of lines of basic stemware. Simple is, of course, always best—and fortunately, ornate isn't Pottery Barn's style. I would avoid the goblets, mainly because they make it difficult to swirl wine properly. Wineglasses with thick stems are also not the greatest, but they'll do, and they have the advantage of being tougher than their slender-stemmed cousins. Pottery Barn also carries a range of ice buckets, wine coolers, and trays in a variety of styles that can help you outfit your wine-loving life in unpretentious style. Just about everything here can be had for less than $100.

williams-sonoma

❊ *110 7th Ave.*
212-633-2203

❊ *1175 Madison Ave.*
212-289-6832

the new york book of wine

The national gourmet retailer just happens to be a good place to stock up on Riedel stemware—the undisputed king of wineglasses. This Austrian company, whose wares Williams-Sonoma carries in both the premium Sommelier series and the more value-priced Vinum line, is famous worldwide among serious wine connoisseurs for its dedication to maximizing wine-drinking pleasure, but also for creating glasses that are customized to individual wine styles. There's a Riedel for just about every wine you can think of, from red Burgundy to Zinfandel and bourbon to tequila. These handblown crystal stems aren't cheap and they aren't durable, but they make wonderful gifts for dedicated wine lovers. Williams-Sonoma also carries a variety of other wine-related paraphernalia.

Corkscrews

In addition to wine and wineglasses, corkscrews are all you really need to launch a lifetime of oenophilia. First off: Get rid of those spread-arm-style numbers and anything that consists of just a "worm" (the screw part) connected to a grip or handle. They're useless and will destroy as many corks as they extract. I favor the famous "waiters friend," a leverage-type folding corkscrew that resembles a pocketknife, but it requires some practice. If a more fail-safe option appeals to you, get a Screwpull. This design extracts the cork simply by the process of inserting the worm and turning. Works every time. If you really get into wine, the indestructible Rabbit works even better—mainly because it involves about half as much effort. It uncorks a bottle of wine like most people uncap a bottle of beer.

buying wine in the big apple

First-time visitors to New York are often surprised to learn that the city is not a vast, undifferentiated megalopolis but rather a large cluster of individual neighborhoods, each with its own distinctive personality. Wine shops in New York are often the same way. It's been said that all politics are local. Well, when it comes to New York, so is wine.

Over time, most New York wine shops have established their own unique customer bases. Astor Wine & Spirits, for example—on the edge of the bohemian East Village—carries a diverse stock of bargain bottles. By contrast, Sherry-Lehmann, on the affluent Upper East Side, is better known for fine Burgundy and Bordeaux. Other shops, notably Union Square Wine & Spirits, located near a downtown hub of activity, aim for inclusiveness, keeping everything from Oregon pinot noir to Japanese sake on the shelves.

A few stores have even decided to focus on the wines of one country. Vino, just north of the Flatiron district, specializes in Italian wines, as does Italian Wine Merchants, farther south. The curiously named Pet Wines, housed on the ground floor of a kennel, is an important resource for lovers of German wine.

The individual entries for wine shops in this book will give you a sense not only of the particular vibe in New York's various wine shops but also of the wines in which those shops specialize. So whether you're on the hunt for a chardonnay from Long Island or a rosé from Provence, you'll be able to find it with ease. Note: A 2003 change in New York state law allows wine stores to be open on Sundays, if they so choose.

wine stores

acker merrall & condit

❋ *160 W. 72nd St.*

212-787-1700

Hours: Monday to Saturday, 9 A.M. to 10 P.M.

What Sherry-Lehmann is to the well-heeled Upper East Side, Acker Merrall & Condit is to the somewhat more honky-tonk Upper West Side. Of course, Acker Merrall isn't exactly Mary Ann to Sherry's Ginger; quite the contrary, Acker Merrall is just as serious and, when you get right down to it, formidable an establishment. It's just that over here on the other side of Central Park, the vibe is a little less formal. The shop itself is, like Sherry, thoroughly not ostentatious, compact even. That is, until you get down to perusing the labels. There are bargains to be had, but that's not really why you come here. No, at Acker Merrall, you're talking about accumulated decades of experience and expertise, in the staff and on the shelves. It's possible that you could zip in here blind and never, ever walk out with a bad bottle. From California pinot noirs to fine red Burgundies, Acker Merrall has staked a clear claim on the hearts and minds of discriminating consumers—just don't pay any attention to the hot dog stand around the corner, which is, by the way, one of the best in the city. Come to think of it, if you ask nicely, the staff at Acker will more than likely suggest the perfect pairing. But please, hold the sauerkraut.

astor wine & spirits

❊ *12 Astor Place*

212-674-7500

Hours: Monday to Saturday, 9 A.M. to 9 P.M.

It's not often, when entering a wine store, that you are immediately presented with the option of grabbing a shopping cart. At Astor, however, customers tend to buy in volume. That's because this venue—which has held its ground on the edge of the East Village through successive waves of gentrification (heroin addicts gave way to punks who gave way to junior partners in law firms and NYU students)—is bargain central. There's more good cheap wine here than almost any place else in town. Most of it is housed in ranks of display cases, arranged so that you can meander up and down the aisles with your aforementioned shopping cart and, well, load up. Although targeted shopping is not a problem, particularly if you're in the wine-drinking vanguard that constantly seeks out the latest bargains from around the world. Astor was into Spanish wines before a lot of other stores, and into South American wines before consumers discovered the robust values of the southern hemisphere, and continues to seek out international bottlings that pack enormous bang for the buck. Which is not to say that wallet-friendly wines are entirely the rule; ample supplies of French, Italian, and California vintages can be found, in a variety of price categories (though often cheaper than at other stores). Just aim your cart in the direction of the hanging neon signs that indicate the country you're interested in. And if you simply stroll in off the street with no particular predisposition, oenophilically, then be sure to hit up the staff, which unlike a lot of the transient service labor in this part of town, is dedicated, courteous, and diligent. They'll help track down whatever you need. But be careful—chances are, even if you just came in for a bottle, you'll leave with a case.

best cellars

✳ *1291 Lexington Ave.*

212-426-4200

Hours: Monday to Thursday, 10 A.M. to 9 P.M. ;

Friday and Saturday, 10 A.M. to 10 P.M.

When Josh Wesson, a hotshot young wine professional, first opened Best Cellars, he probably expected to do a snappy business in a neighborhood that, while fairly affluent, was underserved by good wine stores. It's not as clear whether he imagined that his concept of grouping wines by flavor quality would effectively reinvent the way wines are sold, not just at the retail level but also in restaurants. But Wesson is something of a wine-marketing visionary. Realizing that old-fashioned wine shops, by shelving wines according to region, tended to confuse and intimidate consumers who responded more to taste than geography, Wesson organized his selection according to flavor categories. White were "fresh," "soft," or "luscious"; reds were "juicy," "smooth," or "big." Extra information was supplied by the witty tasting notes that Wesson wrote for each wine. The package was all compellingly presented in a snug simple space designed by David Rockwell, where wines were stored like artillery shells in back-lighted wall slots. It was a browser's paradise for youthful customers who found old-school wine stores, with their wood-shelved confines and knowledgeable but perhaps haughty staffs to be a fusty, bewildering encounter. To make matters even more alluring, Best Cellars started out selling nothing priced higher than $10. The store was a ravishing success, influencing dozens of restaurant wine directors to reorder their own wine lists along the lines of Wesson's innovative categories. Imitators also appeared on the scene, prompting a lawsuit or two. Regardless, Best Cellars has prospered. Nowadays, you can find wines from just about every corner of the wine-making globe.

The cutoff price has risen slightly, as wines worldwide—possibly thanks to Best Cellars' efforts—have risen in cost. The scene here remains very youth-oriented, with just-out-of-college Upper East Side professionals ducking in on their way home from their daily subway commutes. You'll also note that women—frequently discouraged by the decidedly masculine vibe of older shops such as Sherry-Lehmann and Acker, Merrall & Condit—are key customers at Best Cellars. If you want to see the most innovative recent idea in wine at work, this is where you should go.

Is it worth it to age your wine?

The short answer, contrary to the image of the wine connoisseur as nefarious cultural snob, is: No. The vast majority if wine benefits in no way from aging of any sort. In fact, even doing something as seemingly innocuous as leaving a bottle of $15 chardonnay out in your kitchen for more than a few weeks will provoke a significant downturn in that wine's quality. Frankly, when you buy wine and bring it into your house, with few exceptions you should drink it right away. This is not to suggest that wine is a delicate thing; it's actually much tougher than people think. But its toughness, like any perishable, agricultural product, has limits. And chances are that the bottle of Australian Cabernet you picked up at the wine store has already experienced some damaging extremes of temperature, even if it was shipped across the Pacific in a climate-controlled container. But bear this in mind: Most wine produced in the world today is designed to be drunk within a year. Sure, a few hearty reds can probably hold out for a bit longer, but the genuinely ageworthy wines are built to be, for all practical purposes, undrinkable in their youth. In other words, if you plan to age your wines, you need to buy wines that have that potential already engineered into them. So, for the most part, "laying down" wines that you pick up for under $20 is a fool's undertaking. Interestingly, there are some exceptions—and many of them can be found in New York! Finger Lakes Rieslings have all the qualities you would expect in ageworthy wines, for sub-$20 price tags.

the burgundy wine company

✢ *143 W. 26th St.*

212-691-9092

Hours: Monday to Saturday, 10 A.M. to 7 P.M.

Burgundy! Bourgogne! Pinot noir! (And not incidentally, chardonnay, too.) This is the Burgundy Wine Company's claim to fame, its raison d'être as far as its place in the firmament of New York wine stores is concerned. Relocated to a very swank new location just north of Chelsea on the West Side, the establishment is even more obsessively focused on Burgundy and Burgundy-style wines that ever before. The new shop is exceptionally beckoning; it resembles a minimalist's take on the classic Parisian brasserie, with its red storefront and large windows. Inside, the floors are rough, unfinished wood, the art is limited but dramatic, and the wines are arranged in neat, slender, stately—but unpretentious—displays near the entrance. The staff labors in the store's rear, in what looks like a European architecture office or art gallery. Don't be surprised, if, like Italian Wine Merchants, the Burgundy Wine Company is not dependent on walk-in traffic. Their clientele is worldwide, and they sell as much wine by phone, fax, and via the internet as they do the old-fashioned way. You don't get to this level without possessing a vast knowledge and understanding of your region of specialty, and on this score the BWC is second to none. Burgundy is, despite its status among connoisseurs as the Other Great French Wine Region (next to Bordeaux), still a cultish pursuit. Confronting the Burgundy selection at a typical wine store is like trying to read ancient Greek, so baffling are the labels, so difficult is it to sort out a wine's producer from the vineyards from which the grapes were sourced. But rest assured, if a thoroughgoing Burgundy primer is what you're after, the BWC is beyond compare. It should be your first stop—and a place you return to time after time.

chelsea wine vault

❊ *75 9th Ave.*

212-462-4244

Hours: Monday to Friday, 10 A.M. to 9 P.M.;

Saturday, 10 A.M. to 8 P.M.

A wine-lover's bastion on Manhattan's far West Side (the neighborhood used to be better known for taxi garages than art galleries and gourmet grocery stores), this is one big shop, and a wonderful place to get lost after buying breads, meats, and produce at Chelsea Market's other fine-food venues. Located in a former factory, Chelsea Wine Vault really lives up to its name. Upstairs, vast floor space is jammed with thousands of bottles, everything from French Chablis to offbeat Italian whites. Downstairs, in a onetime fallout shelter, there is extensive case-storage for customers who require temperature and humidity-controlled space and also a tasting room in which wine classes can be taught. Customers tend to be more stylish than what you might encounter in Midtown or on the Upper West Side; hard-core oenophiles tend to focus on the store's excellent lineup of often-scarce California wines, especially cabernets, chardonnay, and zinfandels. The stock of Italian wines is also superb. Germans are surprisingly strong, given that they're not a wildly popular category among general consumers (though there's actually no shortage of Riesling nuts in New York), and European shoppers who make their homes in this trendy neighborhood seem to enjoy the shop just as much as the loft-dwelling Americans you would expect to find in here, dressed in Prada and Helmut Lang, loading up on Rioja before heading over to the Barneys Co-op to buy even more Prada and Helmut Lang.

crossroads wine & liquor

❊ *55 W. 14th St.*

212-924-3060

Hours: Monday to Saturday, 9 A.M. to 8:45 P.M.

No, it's not exactly attractive, what with the lurid yellow sign and the liquor-store entrance, located just a few steps from what was, a decade ago, one of New York's most desolate intersections. Inside, the store is pretty much the definition of cramped: It's virtually impossible for two customers to pass each other in one of the charitably named "aisles" (delineated by cases piled almost to the ceiling and by racks and racks of bottles on display). Forget about trying to examine the entire selection while wearing a backpack or carrying groceries. A diet is recommended. In other words, gird yourself for a wine-store experience that fails to reference any retail trends prior to 1973. But so what? If you want to browse one of the finest wine selections not just in New York but, well, the entire country, look no further than this veritable hole in the wall. California enthusiasts will be particularly rewarded by the extensive collections of cabernet, merlot, pinot noir, and chardonnay (among others), with most of the top producers represented. But Europhile wine lovers will also find plenty of delights, as will drinkers who have caught the Australia, South Africa, or New Zealand bugs. Burgundy and the Rhône Valley are especially strong, as is Germany. Bordeaux isn't overwhelming, but Crossroads invariably gets a few lesser growths that are worth checking out before committing to the Big Boys in a dicey vintage. Champagne is jammed in tight against one wall. And yes, there is liquor, including some exotic gins and hard-to-find whiskeys. Of course, one does have to put up with the space, which hasn't seen anything even vaguely resembling a renovation in quite some time, and probably won't, at least for the foreseeable future. But that's all part of the fun. For true-blue New York oenophiles, coming here is a lot like visiting a cruddy old book shop that nonetheless harbors numerous treasures. You come to look and look and look, to read labels and badger the exceptionally well-schooled (and opinionated) staff. They're more than happy to deal with all comers, from Robert Parkerites who consult back issues of *The Wine Advocate* (they're kept on hand) before deciding on a purchase, to no-nonsense customers who enter the store and announce that they're in the market for a "big cheap bottle of Scotch." No, I'm not making that up. It's Crossroads. Anything can happen here.

garnet wines & liquors

✳ *929 Lexington Ave.*

212-772-3211

Hours: Monday to Saturday, 9 A.M. to 9 P.M.

Quite possibly the perfect neighborhood wine store but with the kind of citywide loyalty that only a stupendous selection can inspire. Garnet isn't fancy in the least. In fact, it resembles a college-textbook store more than a wine shop. We're not talking an abundance of weathered wood shelving here, crammed with dusty old bottles. Instead, the completely unromantic, downright industrial lighting gives the place a no-nonsense feel. Of course, this clean, well-lighted shop is your best Upper East Side alternative to Sherry-Lehmann. The breadth of choice is similar, the staff knows what it's talking about—but the prices tend to be a little lower. Sometimes a lot lower. The wines are also more accessible, racked as they are right out in the open. Anything you could possibly imagine, whether you're a rank newcomer to wine or a seasoned pro, can be found here. From high-caliber Spanish Rioja to obscure Alsatian Gewürztraminer, not to mention plenty of everything in between (notably red Burgundy), Garnet has it on hand. Sure, the store's aesthetic puts some in the mind of a wine warehouse, but once you cross the threshold and behold the lineup of reasonably priced Bordeaux, you'll be hooked. In a weird sort of way, the anti–wine shop atmosphere was well ahead of its time. Not too far away, Best Cellars, in the late 1990s, shattered preconceptions about what a wine store is supposed to look like. Garnet was never particularly interested in what a wine store was supposed to look like. The owners always chose to focus on the wine. This has had the unusual effect of making Garnet a real mecca for browsers. Since the environs pose no pressure to make a suitably consummate decision, you can linger for hours, taking it all in. You might feel a touch strange during your first visit, but over time, you'll grow to feel right at home.

Chill your reds and warm your whites

Most people drink their red wines too warm and their white wines too cold. A lot of this has to do with the fact that many wine consumers tend to buy their whites out of the cooler at the wine store. This is always a bad idea, because you have no idea how long the wine has been in there, nor any sense of how cold the cooler actually is (it's almost always too cold). A better tactic is to buy your whites unchilled, then chill them before serving. A half hour in the fridge, or ten to fifteen minutes in the freezer, will do it. The last thing you want is to drink a chardonnay that's forming ice on its surface. You can also dunk the bottle in an ice bucket, but be sure to add cold water to the ice, so that thermodynamics can function properly. If you do happen to come across a too-cool wine, uncork it and allow it to warm for a bit. You'll be rewarded with much more complex flavors and aromatics. As for reds . . . well, they weren't meant to be served at room temperature—at least, not the temperature of most modern rooms. In the good old days, red wines were often drunk in houses that were very cool by contemporary standards. They were also cellared in cool, damp places. Some reds in particular need to be almost crisply cool in order taste their best. Beaujolais Nouveau is perhaps the best example. But so is white zinfandel, rosé, or any sort of blush wine.

grande harvest wines

✳ *33 Grand Central Terminal*

212-682-5855

Hours Monday to Friday, 8 A.M. to 9 P.M.;

Saturday, 10 A.M. to 8 P.M.

New Yorkers often say that living in the city that never sleeps is all about three things: location, location, location. If that's true (and trust me, it is), then Grande Harvest Wines is the best-situated wine store in town. It resides just off the main concourse of Grand Central station. A compact establishment that occupies space once taken up by a theater, the store is almost a wine gallery, encased in glass. The selection here is, accordingly, tightly curated (there simply isn't space for the kind of sprawl found elsewhere). Strengths are in France and California, but the sturdy wooden shelves feature a little bit of everything. Bargains do not exactly abound, but that isn't what Grand Harvest is all about. However, if you're rushing to catch an after-work ride on the New Haven line, and you discover that you're short on wine for dinner, Grande Harvest is a perfect stopover. Don't miss the extensive selection of grappas, an Italian spirit distilled from the last remnants of the wine-making process.

italian wine merchants

❖ *108 E. 16th St.*

212-473-2323

Hours: Monday to Friday, 10 A.M. to 7 P.M.;

Saturday, 11 A.M. to 7 P.M.

For many wine lovers in New York, Italy is the new France. And for those wine drinkers, Italian Wine Merchants is the next best thing to a trip to the Boot. Operated by celebrity chef Mario Batali, his partner (and devoted Italian oenophile) Joseph Bastianich, and Sergio Esposito, who manages the store, Italian Wine Merchants does far less walk-in business than most other Manhattan wine shops. However, if your goal is to educate yourself according to an escalating scale of Italian wine quality—beginning with simple, bargain-priced Chiantis, progressing through the wines of Northern Italy, all the way up to pricey super Tuscans and esoteric whites from regions as far afield as Liguria and Friuli (an IWM specialty, home to the Bastianich's own label)—then this inviting store just off Union Square is hard to beat. Visiting is a lot like traveling to Tuscany; the decor is solid but cheerful, distinguished by dark wood shelving, crisp descriptions of individual wines, and the floors are covered in luxuriously weathered carpets. The staff is uniformly helpful and possessed of great vinous knowledge, not to mention devotion to their jobs (they oughta be devoted—Batali and Bastianich have practically turned Italian wine and food lovers into a minor Manhattan religious sect). When you select a wine for purchase, your order is zipped downstairs to the temperature-and-humidity-controlled storage cellar, and within a few minutes, your bottle arrives via dumbwaiter, a charming old-fashioned touch. In a display case that functions as the checkout counter, IWM also houses a formidable collection of antique corkscrews and assorted wine-related paraphernalia. In the back, shoppers will find a Salumeria, where the IWM crew dries, cures, and ages their own salamis, prosciuttos, and sausages, and also conducts wine-tasting classes and culinary demonstrations. For the avid Italophile stalking the streets of lower Manhattan, Italian Wine Merchants is the kind of place that can develop into an almost daily addiction. Regular customers should take advantage of Joe and Sergio's significant connections to wine producers in Italy to secure cellaring quantities of hard-to-obtain wines.

morrell & co. wines and spirits

❊ *One Rockefeller Plaza*

212-688-9370

Hours: Monday to Friday, 9 A.M. to 7 P.M.;

Saturday, 10 A.M. to 7 P.M.

I always think of Morrell as the New York wine store with the most style and panache. Sherry-Lehmann may have the hard-core Upper East Side oenophiles cornered, and Acker Merrall & Condit may perform the same function across town, but in between these two, in perhaps the most desirable location a wine store could have for foot traffic—a stone's throw from Rockefeller Center's skating rink—resides Morrell & Co, which exudes a refreshing, youthful vibe. Under the exceedingly professional and energetic management of siblings Peter and Roberta Morrell, as well as their partner and auction director Nikos Antonakeas, Morrell has really shown off its passion and verve in the past decade. For starters, the family business, unlike the competition, has a hand in all three aspects of the wine scene in New York: retail, auctions, and restaurants. This last is the brainchild of Antonakeas, who several years ago realized that opening a wine bar, with the wine shop next door, might act as automatic advertisement—and also encourage wine-bar visitors to seek out the wines they had sampled, simply by walking a few feet. There are now two wine bars under Morrell management. Auctions are also an area in which Morrell excels, particularly in the sale of highly collectible red Bordeaux (again, they act as a frisky counterpart to the more staid auction houses, Sotheby's and Christie's). The store itself is snug but sleek and very crisply organized. French wines have pride of place along the right-hand wall, but Antonakeas is a pinot-noir nut, so expect to see plenty of Burgundy, as well as pinots from California and Oregon. And don't assume that just because Morrell is so well-known for moving the expensive stuff that you can't find bargains here. The management makes a point of seeking out wines from all the world's important regions that combine value with quality.

nancy's wines

❊ *313 Columbus Ave.*

212-877-4040

Hours: Monday to Saturday, 10 A.M. to 9 P.M.

For whatever reasons, this extremely—some might say cultishly—well regarded store on the Upper West Side is the absolute beating heart of Riesling connoisseurship in the city. That's not necessarily a great thing to be anywhere but New

York; Riesling isn't exactly America's most beloved wine variety right now (of course, it used to be, back when more Americans drank sweet rather than dry wines). However, New York has never been short of Riesling fanatics, due in large part to the abundance of restaurateurs and sommeliers who have long understood that, of all the world's truly great varietal, Riesling is perhaps the best match for food. It can range in style from fairly dry, crisp, and steely, to—in the form of the borderline unpronounceable Trockenbeerenausleses—syrupy sweet, unctuous, and hypnotically complex. In other words, it is a wine for all seasons, all palates, and all cuisines. Spend enough time around dedicated oenophiles, and you will invariably be indoctrinated into the glories of Riesling—the underappreciated glories. Mind you, there are plenty of folks, many of them Nancy's customers, who like it that way. As long as Riesling remains unpopular vis-à-vis reds from Italy, Australia, and California, the more of it there is for the Riesling- heads. It's not surprising that the Upper West Side, a neighborhood that for decades has prided itself on appreciating a good bargain, is where Nancy's calls home, in a snug, modern little location that stocks many wines besides Riesling (almost all of which are personally annotated by the staff). But back to Rieslings, which offer what's known as a quality-to-price ratio (QPR) that's second to none, particularly the German versions, which show the most sophistication and range. These days, the very trendy region is the Mosel; wines from this area are leaner, sharper, and drier than their counterparts from other justifiably famous and storied sites of vineyard cultivation in Germany. They represent an excellent point of entry for anyone interested in this severely neglected, but undeniably wonderful, grape.

pet wines & spirits

❋ *415 E. 91st St.*

212-987-7600

Hours: Tuesday to Friday 12 P.M. to 9 P.M.; Saturday, 10 A.M. to 9 P.M.; Sunday, 12 P.M. to 9 P.M.

No, this Upper East Side store isn't about getting Rover wasted on cheap red rotgut. Nor is it trying to attract fans of the Beach Boys who also happen to be wine lovers. But it is perhaps the oddest wine shop in the city, if not the whole country. That's because it's owned and operated by the folks behind Run Spot Run, a kennel and "doggie day care" facility next door. But wait. It gets even more unusual. Pet Wines has a thing for Germans. Not shepherds. Wines. Why is this exotic? Mainly due to the minimal popularity of German wines among the American wine-drinking public, which tends to prefer hearty reds. Riesling, the great grape of Germany, makes fantastic wines that often last far longer than, say, California merlot, and furthermore offer lots more complexity for generally reasonable prices. But wine drinkers have not bought into the Germanic bounty (an all the more strange occurrence, as sweeter Rieslings were once just as popular as French reds in New York). Still, Pet Wines remains dedicated, due largely to the efforts of Willie "The Wine Avenger" Glückstern, a Gotham-based Riesling fanatic and importer who acts as a consultant for the shop (he also does work for Manhattan's other German wine Shangri-la, Nancy's Wines). And lest you not take the name seriously enough, just drop by the store any old afternoon and watch the dogs kenneled at Run Spot Run cavort behind a picture window at the rear of the establishment. Apart from that entertaining distraction, you really should give the German wines stocked here a whirl. Not all Riesling is created sweet (though some of the truly great ones are, those with the very, very long names). There are plenty of steely, minerally driven wines of phenomenal depth here, and the staff possesses copious knowledge of all of them. And with the extraordinary 2001 vintage on the shelves, the time to enjoy a life-altering—or at least palate-altering—experience is ripe. Heck, if you have a dog, you could easily become a regular.

The gift of wine

We've all been there. Called upon to attend a birthday, anniversary, or just a cocktail party, we feel the need to bring a gift. Enter wine. Of course, there's a potential problem. Let's say you arrive at the party, present your gift of wine—and then a few hours later spot the empty bottle, tipped over on its side, snuggled down into the carpet amid broken potato chips and beer bottle caps. Not such a great way for a gift to wind up, now is it? You can prevent this from happening by buying wines as gifts that most people have no interest in drinking. I usually favor port or dessert wines, and assume that, after an event, the recipients will take stock and say, "Hey, who gave us the Sauternes?" Beats having your gift prematurely enjoyed—possibly by the wrong person.

sherry-lehmann

❊ *679 Madison Avenue*

212-838-7500

Hours: Monday to Saturday, 9 A.M. to 7 P.M.

Other stores are larger and more impressive, but for a certain breed of New York oenophile—cultured, well traveled, focused on the classics—Sherry-Lehmann is the center of the universe. For decades, the establishment has anchored, with gentility and charm, a stretch of Madison Avenue on the Upper East Side that has recently become well-known as an upscale shopping thoroughfare. The overall coziness of the shop is deceiving; this softly lighted, wood-paneled enclave doesn't look as if it would shelter $10 million worth of wine, much of it consisting of the world's most prestigious bottlings. Almost always bustling, particularly during the holiday season and around Thanksgiving—when the arrival of Beaujolais Nouveau (France's annual answer to soda pop) gives the otherwise prim and efficient staff a chance to loosen up—the real name of the game here is fine Bordeaux and Burgundy. Employees are intimate with blue-chip names such as Latour, Lafite Rothschild and Le Montrachet, but they can also point out buried treasures and reliable values. Fairly oldfangled by comparison with some of new, concept-oriented stores (see Best Cellars) but in possession of the kind of credentials from which both serious collectors and everyday customers can benefit from. And by the way, this might be the best place to buy champagne in the whole city.

union square wine & spirits

✣ *33 Union Square West*

212-675-8100

Hours: Monday to Saturday, 9 A.M. to 9 P.M.

This is the hippest wine store in the city. And the customers prove it. First off, Union Square—a hub of political protest—is an epicenter of the fashion, advertising, media, and dining businesses in New York. The people who live and work in the surrounding Flatiron District lofts like—no, *need*—to consider themselves privy to the newest of the new, the chicest of the chic. And Union Square Wine & Spirits is there to serve their quest for cool when it comes to wine. The store wears its sympathies on its sleeve: almost an entire wall is devoted to California wines, with Italy and Australia commanding prime floor space. The stodgier Old World—France, Germany, et al.—is relegated to the rear. Not that the store doesn't carry some fantastic Bordeaux, Burgundy, and Riesling; quite the contrary, their radar on the best Old World wines tends to be pretty reliable. And trendy, even. I was turned on to a small-production "cult" wine from Bordeaux here, and if the inexpensive but intriguing wines of Beaujolais's Cru vineyards turn you on, they have plenty. (Cru Beaujolais is the Beaujolais region's "real" contribution to wine-making—the soda-poppy Beaujolais Nouveau that Americans have come to love is really just a seasonal wine that's produced, and drunk, in a hurry, not taken very seriously.) Bargains also abound here, and they're usually strategically positioned right at the front of the store. The staff is attentive and . . . well, hip (wine director Steve Gett is a refugee from the music business). No one seems to intimidate them, from glossy magazine editors to architects to Wall Streeters on their way home from the office to supermodels. To be honest, I'm not sure wine is the only reason to go here—you might be able to pick up a date for Saturday night, if you feel like it. And since Union Square Wine & Spirits sponsors countless tastings, some conducted on their comfortably social mezzanine level, you might actually have someplace to go where you can share a passion for wine if you get lucky.

What to do with a half-finished bottle?

There has been a ton of commentary on this question, which arose due to wine's irrevocable tendency to oxidize once uncorked. Some advocate transferring the wine to smaller bottles (known as "half bottles," because they contain exactly half of a standard 750 ml bottle), then recorking these smaller bottles and putting them in the refrigerator. Others recommend pump-sealing systems, as well as sealing systems based on nitrogen gas. I've tried the pump system (known commercially as Vacu-Vin) and can vouch for it; it seems to preserve a partially drained 750 ml for at least a second day—far better, anyway, than simply recorking. I don't like the fridge option myself, for red wines, because I think that temperature fluctuation does more damage to red wine than oxidation. So what's the answer? My feeling is that the average adult couple can get through a bottle of wine in two days, sticking to a healthy regimen of drinking two glasses each, with dinner, over two consecutive evenings. So, in fact, this question shouldn't even come up. Inescapably, an opened bottle of wine is going to decline slightly by day two. But most folks will scarcely notice the change. By day three, you should be on to another bottle. Note that when dealing with a very fine wine, say a nice old Burgundy that you've been cellaring for a decade, it would be absolutely idiotic to do anything other than finish it off. Older wines tend to fall to pieces very rapidly if left open for more than 12 hours (though, obviously, they can benefit greatly from a period of "breathing" before being drunk). Think ahead: If you're a light drinker invite some friends over to share!

vino

✳ *121 E. 27th St.*

212 725-6516

Hours: Monday to Saturday, 12 P.M. to 10 P.M.

East 27th Street, between Park Avenue South and Lexington Avenue, is a vital wine corridor in New York. Not only do the employees of the world's largest wine magazine, *Wine Spectator*, troop to work here at their headquarter's side entrance, but this is where Charles Scicolone and Nicola Marzovilla have based their small culinary and oenophilic empire. Marzovilla is from Puglia, a region in the south of Italy; his restaurant, I Trulli (which is across the street), seeks to deliver unexpurgated the cuisine and wines of this region to New Yorkers. The wine shop that he and Scicolone have established across the street has a slightly broader mandate. Many of the most premium wines of Italy are represented on Vino's low, wood shelves. The emphasis is on quality. Sure, there are affordable wines to be found, especially from Sicily and Sardenia, but the typical Vino customer is on a quest for fine Barolos and Brunellos from, respectively, Piedmont and Tuscany. Vino carries a great selection of these blue-chip offerings, as well as a host of trendy "super Tuscan" wines and even some more exotic bottlings, from regions such as Friuli and Sicily. Wine tastings are held frequently in Vino's suave, modern decor, while a satellite location provides a comfortable setting for wine courses. In classic Italian fashion, it is situated as locally as possible, just a block to the east.

vintage new york

❖ *482 Broome St.*

212-226-9463

Hours: Monday to Saturday, 11 A.M. to 9 P.M.;

Sunday, 12 P.M. to 9 P.M.

At this light-filled Soho shop, open since 2000, the stars of the show are New York's locally produced wines. (It's true, New York state's wine business is booming—but most New Yorkers are completely oblivious to their very own Napa.) Because owners Susan Wine and Robert A. Ransom operate a winery upstate, they are entitled by law to operate a tasting-room and urban retail outpost seven days a week. So even before New York changed its wine-retailing laws, this was the only store where you could buy a bottle on a Sunday. Intrigued by the idea of a cabernet Franc from Long Island's

North Fork, one of America's up-and-coming wine regions? Or how about a high-caliber Riesling from the Finger Lakes? An ice wine from the Hudson Valley? This is the place. Best of all, one can sample everything on sale at the wine-tasting bar in back. A variety of artisanal products—from cheeses to pâtés—are also available for picnickers on their way to a weekend concert in Central Park. Regular wine-tastings and wine-education classes are offered in the downstairs studio. A second store recently opened on the Upper West Side.

Chapter Five

on the road to oenophilia

back to school: wine classes

Let's face it: Wine can be intimidating. And when intimidated, it never hurts to learn as much as you can about your adversary. Fortunately, New York—in addition to being home to half a dozen fine universities—is also a great place to be if you want to graduate from merely drinking wine to actually studying it.

Like just about everything else in New York, wine courses are run by people with their own distinctive styles. So it's worth it to do some research before committing. The programs listed here aren't cheap, but they are generally acknowledged, by the vinocenti, to be the best. Countless graduates have not only gone on to impress their friends and relatives with newfound expertise, they've advanced to actual careers in the wine world.

This is the internet age, so naturally, most wine courses maintain a Web site. But don't limit your research to an hour of Web surfing. In my view, it's better to ask around. Call up the wine pro who runs the program and quiz him about what you'll be getting. Will there be a lot of tasting? Or will the course focus on basic instruction first and turn to drinking wine later? Is the class designed for aspiring sommeliers? Or simply those curious sorts who would like to improve their personal knowledge?

Also, seek word-of-mouth. The truest test of how good a course will ultimately be is how many graduates roam the world talking up the virtues of the instructor and the pleasure of the experience. Then hit the books. And don't hang out in the back of the class!

Most wine courses are organized in a linear, regional

fashion. You start out with simple white wines, from around the world, then work your way through more complex reds and generally conclude with fortified wines and sometimes champagne and sparkling wines. Actual tastings typically take place after a seminar on a particular wine style or region. Many courses also require a textbook of some sort (usually written by the person leading the classes!) and will furnish graduates with a certificate on completion.

andrea immer at the french culinary institute

❊ *The French Culinary Institute*
462 Broadway
888-FCI-CHEF
www.frenchculinary.com
Fundamentals of Wine, offered twice yearly, spring and fall.
Great Wine and Food Made Simple, offered once yearly, fall.
$895 per person.

Andrea Immer cut her wine-pro teeth under the careful tutelage of Kevin Zraly. She was his protégé and, for a number of years, ran the wine program at Windows on the World. Briefly, she even co-hosted a drinks-oriented show, *Quench*, on the Food Network. After a stint as the beverage director for the hip and youthful Starwood Hotels chain (which boasts several properties in New York), Immer published a pair of books, one a superb basic primer based on her own studies for the prestigious Master Sommelier certification; and the other a food-and-wine-matching guide drawn from her new gig as the Wine Diva—her official title is the stately Dean of Wine Studies—at New York's French Culinary Institute. Immer's courses here are devoted to demystifying wine and concentrating on the key sommelier skill of matching wine with foods. Her plucky, irreverent manner—honed as the wine columnist for *Esquire* magazine—serves her well in these tasks, as does the setting, which after all, is an institution dedicated to the advancement of culinary talent. The Fundamentals course is offered twice yearly and concentrates on treating students as if they were budding restaurant professionals, while the wine-and-food course deals with what is for some the great gustatory challenge of our times. Best of all, students get to put their education to work here—after class they are entitled to a 50 percent discount at FCI's highly regarded teaching restaurant, L'Ecole.

executive wine seminars

❉ *Warwick Hotel, 65 W. 54th St.*

800-404-WINE

www.ewswine.com

The "Ultimate Introduction to Wine" course is $250 per person.

Some of you may not want to commit two entire months to a basic wine course. Executive Wine Seminars, around since 1981, might have just the ticket for you. They offer superb two-day sessions in which you'll be exposed to examples of many significant wine styles, but examples that are also in and of themselves great wines. Like, Bordeaux first growths. Grand cru Burgundies. Stuff on that order. This means that Executive Wine Seminars doesn't pitch itself at the average Joe; they proudly list the high-flying, New York–based media and financial firms (ABC News, anybody?) that have made use of their services. They also provide customized courses and a special class on cheese. Their goal is to increase the level of confidence with which the typical harried executive approaches wine. Class sizes are kept small, and, for the quality of wines you get to sample, the price represents—to borrow a phrase from Wall Street—a strong buy.

harriet lembeck's wine & spirits program

✼ *New School Adult and Continuing Education*
Wine classes meet at 203 E. 29th St.

212-229-5600

www.nsu.newschool.edu

Contact the New School for information regarding
schedule and fees.

Harriet Lembeck, along with her husband Bill, teaches a fairly low-key but still comprehensive and intense course. Their classroom is snug, to put it charitably, so chances are you'll meet somebody in class and get to know him. Lembeck lacks Zraly's inimitable chutzpah, and she can't quite match Immer's spunkiness, but she covers plenty of ground and makes considerable use of visual aids (even though she sometimes fails to make eye contact during her lectures). She also uncorks some pretty tasty wines, from fine champagne to single-vineyard Rhône reds. Lembeck also maintains some academic cred: She's on the faculty at the New School, and has under her belt one of the definitive wine guides for amateurs and professionals alike, *Grossman's Guide to Wines, Beers, and Spirits*. But perhaps her greatest claim to fame is her unique style of aerating wines when she tastes: Nary a student graduates from her course without being able to do a passable imitation of Lembeck's signature slurp.

the institute of culinary education at peter kump

✼ *50 W. 23rd St.*

212-847-0700

www.iceculinary.com

The wine-and-spirits program here at the Institute of Culinary Education offers a wide variety of courses, for everyone from the absolute beginner to the worldly sophisticate looking to bone up on the wines of a particular region. Director Ron Ciavolino teaches the six-session Wine Essentials course, which will probably interest most newcomers (and, at $435, it's about half as costly as some of the city's other long-term courses). Ciavolino also leads a quickie, two-session introductory course, for $125, that's designed to provide a wealth of wine knowledge for the time-challenged. From there, it's all about specialization. There are one-session courses on Bordeaux, Burgundy, and wine-and-food matching (this last one makes sense, actually, as Peter Kump is a first-class cooking school). An added benefit of ICE's wine programs is the high caliber of wine pro that leads classroom discussions, in the school's new wine-education facility. You might get your info on Burgundy from Daniel Johnnes, the dean of Burgundophiles in New York and the wine director at, among other New York restaurants, the venerable Montrachet in Tribeca. The ubiquitous Willie Glückstern also does duty here, contributing to the wine-and-food sessions.

international wine center

✳ *1113 Broadway, Ste. 520 (classes are taught at the New York Institute of Technology and other locations)*

212-627-7170

www.learnwine.com

It's best to consult the Center's Web site for a description of the many courses available.

Expensive, thorough, and not for the faint of heart. If you aspire to someday become, oh, I don't know, a Master Sommelier or Master of Wine, this is the program for you. Hard to say that a friendly, collegial vibe rules the day here. More like an intense, wine-geek-in-training ethos. A serious wine-education option, for people who think that course titles like Intermediate Certificate IC303 succinctly capture the mood of what they're after. That course is the basic intro deal, at $617, running for about a month and a half in the evenings. But that's just the beginning. Who knows where your time at the IWC will take you? There's an advanced diploma program that requires a two-year commitment. Instructors here are not 0

the celebrity wine-pro sort; rather, they are drawn from the ranks of dedicated wine-industry folk around the city. The president of the IWC is Mary Ewing-Mulligan, a Master of Wine who, with her husband, Ed McCarthy, is responsible for the wildly popular *Wine for Dummies* books.

kevin zraly's windows on the world wine course

✳ *Marriott Marquis Hotel*

   1535 Broadway

   845-255-1456

   www.windowsontheworldwineschool.com

   Two seasonal, eight-week, two-hour evening courses

   per year, spring and fall.

   $895 per person.

Zraly is possibly the best-known sommelier in all New York, if not the world. The now sadly—and tragically—destroyed Windows on the World wine cellar, housed in what was the World Trade Center, was his baby. Drawing on its resources, high above lower Manhattan, he educated an entire generation of wine pros, future sommeliers, and enlightened amateurs. Zraly's course—after a period of mourning, he resumed teaching it at the Marriott Marquis hotel in Times Square—is all about personality. The man can imbue more energy into a discussion of Puligny-Montrachet than some statesmen can the fate of the European Union. His enthusiasm is infectious; by the time the eight-week course has concluded, you will have become not just a wine lover, but a wine acolyte—a crusader for the virtues of the vine. In fact, so thoroughly indispensable has the Windows course become that the textbook Zraly eventually generated out of it, *The Windows on the World Complete Wine Course: A Lively Guide*, has been adopted by many experts as the definitive ABCs-of-wine guide. There are something like two million in print. Zraly is also in great demand as a speaker on wine and as a corporate consultant. As wine courses go, this one is the blue-chip standard by which all others are judged. It's also a relative bargain at the $900 price tag, as students will taste several thousand dollars worth of tremendously desirable wine.

tastings with willie glückstern, "the wine avenger"

❊ *The Park Central Hotel*

870 Seventh Ave. at 56th St.

212-724-3030

www.winesforfood.com

Tastings are held in the evenings, throughout the year.

$250 per person for the series of five.

Glückstern is one of those "only in New York" personalities. An opinionated author (his book, *The Wine Avenger*, pretty much lays out where he's coming from), an in-demand wine consultant (he's composed the wine lists for a number of popular Manhattan restaurants), and an avid educator, he brought himself to extreme local attention by getting married in the cheese department of Zabar's gourmet shop on the Upper West Side. His wine courses and tasting seminars are, as you might imagine, forums in which he presents his unexpurgated theories about wine and food. You can catch him at the Institute of Culinary Education or at any of his $65 one-off tastings.

tastings

regular restaurant and wine-store tastings

It's advisable to keep an eye peeled at all times for wine tastings in wine stores and for special wine dinners at restaurants. In the case of the former, importers and distributors are forever sending their representatives out into the retail marketplace, bearing free samples in the hope that you'll like what you taste and bring a bottle home. In the case of the latter, restaurants will often schedule wine dinners when, for example, a wine-maker is passing through town, promoting his or her wines. The best way to hear about these events before they happen is to get yourself on the mailing lists of whatever wine stores you frequent, and whatever restaurants you dine at that have strong wine programs. Otherwise, you can simply ask around. Staffers at wine shops are always delighted to let customers know about in-store tastings, and restaurateurs think of wine dinners as a great way to fill up large tables and special rooms with customers who pay for the meal and their wines in advance.

what's in a note? many things...

Wine critics have always written notes on the wines they taste, and so should you. Notes are a great way to keep track of your impressions, especially on wines that are entitled to some pretention—that is to say, fine and rare wines of reputation that you might get to taste only once or twice in a lifetime. Mind you, it's not necessary to try to find hints of black olive and smoke in that cabernet sauvignon, much less gooseberries or cat urine (I'm not making that up) in New Zealand sauvignon blanc (and don't even get started on old red Burgundy, in which cow-manure aromas are considered a sign of good breeding). Just note whether you thought the wine was rich or thin, ripe or unripe, fruity or lean. I like to take note of how fresh and acidic a wine is. A very famous, now deceased, British wine writer, Auberon Waugh, always talked about whether a wine was "sweet"—and he didn't mean sugary. It was his personal word for a certain beckoning fullness on the palate. Come up with that kind of thing: your own personal tasting-note language. Keep all your notes together, in a notebook or a computer and just see how often you yank them out. You'll be surprised.

what's blind tasting?

Professional wine critics prefer to taste wines blindly. This means that, before they taste their way through a lineup of, for instance, New Zealand pinot noirs, they'll remove the corks and foil capsules from the bottles, then place the wine in coded paper bags or cloth sacks that conceal the labels. They do this in order to remain as objective as possible. Typically, however, a taster will have at least some idea of what he or she is tasting, often broken down in terms of wine type and region, Italian Sangiovese, for example, or Spanish Rioja. Additionally, prior to tasting through a "flight," a critic will usually sample a previously scored benchmark wine, to "set" his or her palate. Less frequently, if a critic knows he's going to be tasting Alsatian wines, he'll calibrate his palate with a preparatory tasting, just to get used to the Alsatian style of wine-making. Less common is the so-called "double blind" tasting, in which a taster is confronted with bagged, unidentified wines and asked to judge them, without the benefit of even basic information. This challenging type of tasting is the basis for those comedy sketches in which a snooty connoisseur will take a sip of some fusty old wine and proceed to name the winery, the year, and detail the pluses and minuses of the vintage. ("The weather was excellent in June, but rains interrupted the harvest and the vintner struggled during the year with his divorce and an inopportune recurrence of gout.") Blind tasting is, quite honestly, the best way to judge wines. And anyone who has access to a stack of brown paper lunch bags and a Magic Marker can give it a try. It is not, however, the be-all and end-all of tasting. Some great critics consider it more useful when the taster is performing a consumer service, rather than, say, assessing a vertical of Château Latour. In my own tasting, I do it about half the time (when I was at *Wine Spectator*, I officially did it all the time—the magazine's policy is to taste everything blind, no exceptions). But I also taste plenty of wine without blinding myself. In the end, if you aren't assigning scores to wines, I don't think it's necessary.

what to eat and drink when you taste?

Evidently, some wine lovers like to taste wines with a clear, unencumbered palate—the better to focus on a wine's particular qualities. Not me. I like to have a little something to nibble on while I taste. The classic is some sort of dry, relatively flavorless, unsalted cracker. There are some that are specially designed and marketed for this purpose, as wine biscuits or a similar designation. To me, a lot of these are too sweet. I've also seen a flavored version that make an attempt to be "pairable" with wines. A gimmick! Matzoh crackers are usually a safe, cheap bet, but even Triscuits or Wheat Thins are okay (just don't gobble them down, as the salt will eventually get to you). At a lot of what are known as "trade" tastings—which are open only to retailers, merchants, restaurateurs, and the press—you'll often find what I consider to be nirvana: a big table piled with cheeses and breads (and occasionally even items like salami and dried sausages). This is great, as the tasting of wine can genuinely benefit from having other flavors in one's mouth. This is especially true where powerfully tannic red wines are concerned; a little, say, roast beef or cheese can harmonize the harsh edges and give a taster a better sense of what the wine will be like once it's calmed down. And here's a tip: If you ever find yourself at a port tasting, keep an eye out for salty cheeses, such as Roquefort or good old blue cheese. They provide an excellent counterpoint to sweet, highly alcoholic fortified wines. As for what you should drink when you taste, I personally favor a lightly effervescent sparkling water (not seltzer, which is too fizzy). The bubbles scour and refresh my palate. But by all means, leave out the slice of lemon or lime. And never, ever drink anything acidic, like fruit juice, when you taste.

to spit or not to spit?

The eternal question. Obviously, when it comes to tasting wine, you need to sniff and you need to swirl. But do you need to spit? After all, the pros do it, sometimes with tremendous brio (I'm a pretty hard spitter myself, I like a powerful stream). The answer is: No, you do not absolutely need to spit. However, if you are (1) driving or (2) hoping to keep your wits about you after more than a dozen or so gulps, spitting is recommended. Also, a condition called "palate fatigue" will frequently set in if you swallow everything and at a far more rapid pace than had you been spitting (if you're tasting hefty reds, you'll get palate fatigue anyway, so you want to keep it at bay for as long as possible). My own policy is to spit everything out except wines from excellent vintages, extremely old wines that take longer to reveal themselves in the mouth, and hard-to-find wines, such as the so-called "cult" cabernets from California. But all the rest wind up in the spit bucket (when it comes to lighter whites, like German Rieslings, I can taste and spit pretty much all day long). This raises another question: What do I use as my spittoon? You can use anything, really, from a 7-Eleven Big Gulp cup to a sterling silver amphora. Me, I like to taste while standing up or walking around, so I favor a deep sink. By the way, in some personal cellars, there are special stone or concrete sinks set up for just this purpose—unlike aluminum spitoons, when you spit into them, they don't splatter. Oh, and here's another tip: Should you ever be fortunate enough to be asked to taste wines directly from barrels in a winemakers cave, it's perfectly acceptable to spit in the floor. Out of courtesy, however, aim for the drains, if you can.

Toothpaste: The wine taster's enemy

A lot of professionals like to taste wine in the morning, when they feel that their palates are sharper. I'm not sure I agree with that, but it does create a problem if you go that route. Should you brush your teeth? Wine can stand up quite ably to almost anything except the sort of ferocious mint flavor found in most American toothpastes (though it's sensible to avoid a cup of coffee or tea right before tasting wine). When wine encounters hyperminty Crest, it's akin to drinking orange juice right after brushing: an unpleasant experience. Several years ago, when I was at *Wine Spectator*, a colleague insisted on early morning tastings. I don't like to leave the house without brushing my teeth, so I was in a quandary. Should I sacrifice oral hygiene for the sake of my career? Or simply go to work with halitosis? It was solved for me by some friends who were living in Italy. They brought back some licorice-flavored toothpaste that was superb for brushing, but that didn't leave a wine-obliterating aftertaste. Thereafter, I demanded that they bring as many tubes as they could get their hands on whenever they came for a visit. Eventually, I found that Tom's of Maine produces a fennel-flavored toothpaste, which could suffice in a pinch. And a friend in the wine business introduced me to another Italian brand (the Italians make the best toothpaste) whose mint aftertaste was so subdued that it wore off in about a half and hour.

what does the 100-point scale mean?

If you buy a lot of wine, especially at New York wine stores, you are going to see a lot of numbers. This is because the two most prominent wine publications in the world, *Wine Spectator* and *The Wine Advocate*, both use the 100-point scale when evaluating wines. The 100-point scale was introduced by *The Wine Advocate*'s Robert M. Parker, Jr., and has been widely adopted as the journalistic standard. Parker says that he went to 100-point scale because he found it more flexible than the old British 20-point scale, and because he felt it would speak to American consumers, who were accustomed to 100-point scales from being graded in school. Some wine writers—notably *The New York Times*' Frank J. Prial—despise the scale and have endorsed a simpler five-star approach. Of course, it's important to note that the 100-point scale is actually a 40-point scale, as you never see a wine that scored a 32 (in practice, these days you never see a wine that scores below 70). Naturally, this has led to charges of grade-inflation, as consumers have been trained to ignore wines that score below 85. Which means that the 100-point scale has, in the eyes of some, been reduced to a 15-point scale, which is five points less broad than the allegedly limited British 20-point scale it was meant to replace. (And sure, you can make the counterargument that the Brit scale was really a 10-point scale, since who would give a wine a 2, but the problem remains that if the Parker/*Spectator* scale is a 15-pointer, and the Brit a 10-pointer, then you only gain five points of flexibility with the bigger scale. To make matters worse, British critics will often insist that scores should be treated with skepticism, and that it's the notes that matter, but that's another kettle of fish.) Regardless of how you do the numbers, the issue persists: How should I interpret the scores? My advice is this: If you encounter a 90-plus-point wine for under $20, grab it. Chances are good that it truly is "outstanding"—and an outstanding value, to boot. Otherwise, look to the numbers around 85, but be wary of $30-plus wines that score in the low 80s. At the moment, the most fertile territory for genuinely good wines, from all parts of the world, is the 85–90 range, especially wines from Europe, whose wines tend to be judged more strictly than New World wines. Remember as well that a weak Euro can make a French 88-pointer seem more expensive than a California wine that received the same score but in fact, might be a more interesting buy. An important tip: Even though a wine that scores in the 70s is supposed to be acceptable and unflawed, you can pretty much bet that the guy or gal who tasted it was unimpressed. And with so much good wine out there right now, life is too short for 77-pointers.

storing wine

New Yorkers suffer a significant disadvantage when it comes to stocking up on wine: Where to put it? This is, after all, the city of the 150-square-foot. studio apartment. Unfortunately, wine, while not exactly fragile, can be ruined if stored in conditions that are too extreme. The key is avoid the two things that wine hates: heat and sunlight. Some more well-heeled oenophiles purchase temperature-controlled storage units, such as EuroCaves, to act as miniature cellars in their digs, but a cool, dark corner of a closet will work just as well. As long as the temperature doesn't fluctuate dramatically, remaining under 65 degrees for most of the year, the wine will be happy next to shoes and boots. Bottles should always be stored on their sides, so that their corks don't dry out. More avid collectors will probably want to investigate the city's numerous case-storage options, many of which are operated by more prestigious wine stores, such as Sherry-Lehmann and Morrell & Co.

the auction scene

(and other valuable tasting opportunities around town)

Once you've gotten relatively proficient at learning your way around wine in New York, you might very well start thinking about obtaining some really collectible juice. If that's the case, I salute you: You've entered a while new realm of wine connoisseurship, one that's so New York it'll probably surprise you.

There are major wine auction houses in Europe, and wine auctions are commonly held on the West Coast, but the majority of the significant auctions occur in New York, in three main venues: Christie's, their rival auction house Sotheby's, and the relative newcomer Morrell & Co.

Auctions are advanced stuff but not hard to get in on. You essentially pay a fee to register as a bidder, receive the auction catalog, and should you attend the actual auction—or even bid via telephone or online—and become the high bidder, you win. Then you part with your money, pay a commission to the auction house, and take possession of your wine. Anyone who has ever bought or sold anything on eBay can handle it (they auction wines there, too, by the way.) Just remember to take a shower and get dressed if you're headed to an auction at Sotheby's.

Auction houses in New York have put a fair amount of effort into maintaining their rare-wine departments. So much, in fact, that celebrity wine specialists—and veritable auction-podium celebrities—have been thrown up. At Christie's, the Grand Old Man of the wine department is Englishman Michael Broadbent. At Sotheby's, Englishwoman Serena Sutcliffe. (Yes, because the auction business transferred from London to New York, it seems at times as if you aren't a real auction house unless your wine maven is British.)

Auction houses are fastidious about gauging the quality of the wines they acquire and sell. Their experts, in much the same way fellow employees would evaluate silver or paintings, examine the wines that are scheduled to be auctioned and judge whether they are in top condition.

Even for the casual wine drinker—who happens to have a little extra cash—auctions can be a great way to obtain wine to drink, not just collect. Often, buying wines at auction is a way to snare, for example, older vintage port that is ready to be uncorked right now. The alternative is to always pay top dollar for fine wines but then be forced to age them yourself, taking on the risk of cellaring and keeping the wines in good shape.

If, however, you go through the auction market, you can buy wonderful older wines, ready to drink (in some cases) as soon as you buy them, that somebody else has taken care of, and whose excellent condition has been confirmed by experts. You can even spend your wine money more effectively this way, locating wines from older vintages whose prices have gone down, relative to other wines, or to what they cost when they were first released. Just remember that wines are typically not auctioned as single bottles; most of the time, you'll be buying at least six. (Although "mixed lots," as jumbled-up groupings of wines are known, can deliver the best bang for the buck of all, especially if drinking is your goal rather than collecting.)

Maybe outbidding an investment banker for a case of 30-year-old Bordeaux doesn't interest you, but the wines themselves do. If this is where you are, New York's auction houses offer what is perhaps the best educational bargain in town. For a small fee, you can attend the pre-auction public tastings.

These events are held so that collectors can get a sneak peek at what they might want to buy later at auction. The tastes are tiny, but where else are you going to have access to, say, a vertical of Opus One, the very expensive wine produced in collaboration by Robert Mondavi and the Rothschilds? Just remember that wine of extreme rarity or special pedigree tends to run out fast, so try to have a tasting plan before you get started. It's no fun to fantasize all day about a drop or two of Screaming Eagle, only to arrive at the tasting once the impossible-to-find California cult wine has all been finished.

christie's

❋ *20 Rockefeller Plaza*

212-636-2000

www.christies.com

Christie's is one pillar of the pair that has dominated the wine-auction scene in New York since the city became as big an auction town as London. Sotheby's is the other. Both work essentially the same territory: fine collectible reds, usually from France, but sometimes—more recently, anyway—from California. Auctions are held around the world. The best way to keep track of when they're being conducted in New York is to periodically check the house's Web site.

morrell & co.

❋ *665 11th Ave.*

212-307-4200

www.morrellwineauctions.com

The young Turk in the New York auction game has certainly not allowed its inexperience with this side of the wine scene to dampen either its ambition or enthusiasm. Auctions have been held for wines that have carried staggeringly pre-auction estimates of value—we're talking close to $10 million—mostly for rare older Bordeaux.

Decanting: myth or necessity?

Few rituals confuse wine newbies as thoroughly as decanting. Let's be frank: It's almost never necessary. Most of the time, it's just fine to pull a cork and pour; these days, the vast majority of wines are filtered prior to bottling, so there won't be any sediment to deal with. The exceptions are older red wines, especially vintage port, and wines that have been intentionally bottled "unfiltered." These can throw a considerable sediment. Simply decant them into a vessel of sufficient volume to handle the entire bottle (anything from a fine crystal decanter to a large canning jar will do, as long as it's clean). Perform the deed by slowly pouring the wine, at an angle, into the decanter, being careful to retain sediment in the bottle. Some seasoned oenophiles use a candle or flashlight so that they can see the sediment. If you like, you can serve the wine from the decanter, or "double decant" the decanted wine back into the bottle, after it has been rinsed of sediment.

sotheby's

�֍ *1334 York Ave.*

212-606-7000

www.sothebys.com

Sotheby's is tucked away on Manhattan's Upper East Side (almost by the East River). As with crosstown rival Christie's, the name of the game here is fine old Bordeaux, but frequent auctions of rare wines can feature California cabernet, port, and even collectible Italian and Spanish wines. As with Christie's, check the Web site frequently to stay abreast of the auction schedule.

making a weekend of wine

new york wine country

Yes, New York makes wine, too. And Californians may be loath to admit it, but until relatively recently, New York state was numero uno as far as U.S. wine production goes (it's currently number two). Was the wine any good? Well, let's just say it was a mixed bag. Since New York's climate (freezing winters, humid summers) isn't exactly as favorable to grape-growing as California's, the so-called "noble" varietal, vinis vinifera, took longer to gain a foothold here. Prior to that, much of the state's output came from hardy native varietal and French hybrids. These grapes yielded a lot of wine, but most of it couldn't stack up very well against what was coming out of Europe or what eventually began to come out of California. In the past twenty years, however, wine-making in New York has entered a new phase. So long, Pink Catawba! Hello, Riesling and merlot.

There are three main wine-making regions in New York state. Two, Long Island and the Hudson Valley, are within relatively easy daytripping distance of New York City. The Finger Lakes is significantly farther away, but it is rife with cozy bed and breakfasts, and can also be reached by plane in about an hour (Jet Blue flies from JFK to nearby Rochester).

In some respects, New York always stood better than a fighting chance at developing a truly modern wine industry; a wealth of knowledge had already been amassed about what kinds of grape did best in the state's three main viticultural regions. Since the 1990s, Long Island has taken the lead in terms of marketing itself to consumers, but the Finger Lakes—which is really New York's most venerable and evolved region—is catching up fast. The Hudson Valley seems, for the moment, a bit adrift, but it's probably only a matter of time before that changes. Because, to borrow a line from the song, if you can make wine here, you can make it anywhere.

❋ long island, the north fork

Of New York's main wine regions, this narrow finger of land, jutting 100 miles into the Atlantic Ocean, bordered by the Peconic Bay to the south and Long Island Sound to the north, is the big story in the state's wine business. Simply put, this is where the buzz is. This is where the big money is being spent to turn former potato fields into productive vineyards. This is where the French wine-making consultants point their private jets. Altogether, there are more than two dozen wineries here, almost all with tasting rooms. It's astounding progress, given that the Long Island wine industry has only been around since the early 1970s (it's about as old as New Zealand's). If you're feeling strong, you can take in most of the wineries in a single day—they're spaced out fairly regularly along the Main Road. But bring some cash. Almost everybody has caught on to the tasting-room hustle and started charging for the pleasure (you'll typically be confronted by a per-flight fee, ranging anywhere from $5 to $15 for three to five wines, more for reserve wines produced in limited quantities).

Long Island has, for the most part, placed its faith in merlot as the grape that will deliver a bright and prosperous future. The reason for this, as many of the region's vintners will tell you, is that the North Fork is on roughly the same latitude as Bordeaux, where some of the world's finest merlot-based wines are produced. Of course, Bordeaux is a borderline wine-making region; a good vintage is determined mainly by the weather. Ditto the North Fork, where a long growing season—usually one that stretches warmly into October, without any rainfall—is required for merlot to shine. This has happened several times in the past ten years, notably in 2001, but just because the North Fork's wine-makers get terrific fruit, doesn't mean they'll be able to transform it into fabulous wine. For the better part of its history, the region has been held back by a lack of wine-making talent. Perfectly satisfactory fruit was oaked into an early grave by inexperienced vintners who had fallen in love with American barrels, a result of a perceived market for woody wines made in a California style. Too often, a nice, lively Long Island merlot shone for its first years of life, then quickly degenerated into a resinous disaster as weak fruit was overwhelmed by heavy-handed oak.

Lately, wine-makers have come to understand that American oak is a powerful thing that needs to be used in moderation. They have also learned the virtues to mellower—but more expensive—French oak barrels. Their viticulture has also improved, as has the age of their vines. And a few producers have abandoned merlot altogether, opting to focus instead on Cabernet Franc, which some believe is the grape that will really make Long Island great. All these factors have, in the past five years, conspired to usher in a new era for North Fork winemaking. Now, if the region's winemakers can just give up on cabernet sauvignon and pinot noir.

Note: General information about the region's wine industry can be found through the Long Island Wine Council, www.liwines.com. And unless otherwise indicated, wineries are located on the Main Road, Route 25.

bedell cellars

631-734-7537

www.bedellcellars.com

Kip Bedell is the namesake of this well-known winery on the Main Road. And it's due largely to his wine-making talent, especially with merlot, Long Island's signature varietal, that Bedell has such a great reputation. Several years ago, Bedell sold out to Michael Lynne, a New York–based film producer, who proceeded to revamp the winery while still keeping Bedell in charge of the winemaking. The result is a much more airy and sophisticated tasting room than what Bedell veterans were used to. The old facility was rustic and barnlike, while the new one seems filled with light—the better to illuminate Lynne's world-class collection of contemporary art. However, unlike some other new wineries, which borrow from European motifs, the face-lifted Bedell Cellars seeks to emulate the dominant architectural modes of Long Island's East End. Well, regardless of your take on the winery's design, there's no disputing its popularity—if anything, Lynne should have figured a bigger parking lot into the renovation, so jam-packed is the current space nearly every weekend in spring and fall. It remains a must-stop, however, as Bedell's touch with merlot remains definitive, the standard to which everyone else on the North Fork should aspire. His roster of wines runs from the basic, everyday Main Road red, straight up to the $30 merlot reserve. Now, that's not exactly a bargain, given that Long Island merlots can be a bit temperamental, depending on the vagaries of weather. But bear in mind that Bedell isn't a California or Australian superproducer, cranking out gallons of juicy, jammy wine. They only do about 8,500 cases per year here, red and white. On Long Island, such limited production means that, in order to continue to beef up quality, they must charge a decent price for what they consider to be their premium wines. If you take into account the amount of wine that gets sold out of the tasting room alone each year, it seems that Bedell's supporters are happy to pay for the pleasure.

castello di borghese
vineyard & winery

❖ Route 48 (Sound Avenue and Alvah's Lane)
Cutchogue, New York
631-734-5111
www.castellodiborghese.com

Well, this is where it all began, in 1973—the Long Island Wine industry. Louisa Hargrave has written a book about the adventure of starting up a winery, but for the Italian prince, Marco Borghese, who purchased the property in 1999, the adventure has just begun. The stars of the show here, wine-wise, are their region's signatures: chardonnay and merlot. Reserve bottlings of both mean that North Fork fans can find real quality.

What the heck is a microclimate?

Spend enough time around wine and wine-makers, and eventually you'll hear someone mention a microclimate. So what is that, exactly? Well, generally speaking, wine grapes are very sensitive little suckers. They're influenced by a whole host of factors, from the kind of soil their vines were grown in (Sandy? Loamy? Rocky?) to the terrain itself (Hilly? Mountainous? Flat?) to more meteorological concerns, such as how many days the sun shone between April and October to how much rain fell in August. Obviously, among all these factors, weather is perhaps the most important, because nothing screws up a vintage quite like bad weather, while nothing makes a brilliant year quite like the weather that causes wine-makers to gaze daily skyward and smile. Now, almost every defined wine-growing region in the world possesses its own unique microclimate, which determines the sort of grape quality you're likely to find there, not to mention advises wine-makers on what varieties of grapes to plant in the first place. For example, many regions in California make rich, fruity red wines because of (1) very little rain; (2) endless sunshine during the growing season; and (3) cool nights, which force the vines to "shut down" for a period of time, thus lengthening the growing season and allowing for higher levels of ripeness. However, as with many things in life, proximity to water makes a difference. In New York state, the Finger Lakes region, due to large glacial lakes that act as giant heat repositories, grapes can get in a reasonable growing season, in a part of the country where heavy winter snows and damp, chilly springs are familiar. Long Island, on the other hand, enjoys a maritime microclimate, with its weather affected largely by the Atlantic Ocean (and yes, that means the occasional hurricane). Microclimates are exotic, surprising deals, but when you're in the middle of one, trying to make wine for a living, you learn to appreciate their prickly personalities.

galluccio family wineries

631-734-7089

www.gristinawines.com

Vince Galluccio is a hefty former telecommunications executive who has invested heftily in this property, formerly known as Gristina. When Galluccio purchased the estate in 2000, he paid $5.5 million—at that point, the highest price for a Long Island winery. He immediately set about making improvements to both the winery's viticulture and its enology, including the hire of the well-traveled and justifiably famous French wine-maker and merlot specialist Michel Rolland as a consultant. Galluccio was fortunate in that Gristina already had one of the best wine-making facilities in the region; prior to arrival of Raphael, it probably was the most technologically advanced. The wine-making team here is an unusual and borderline eccentric bunch. They favor a sort of Franco-American hybrid in the styles of wine they produce. Wine-maker Bernard Cannac and vineyard manager Bernard Ramis, both French, favor a style that is crisply acidic rather than full-blown and fruity—a lucky thing, as the North Fork isn't exactly Napa when it comes to weather (which isn't to say that they can't also produce powerful wines; they can but the sort of monster reds generated in California and Australia just isn't their forté). Galluccio's output consists of juicy merlots, a certain amount of cabernet sauvignon, and chardonnay that fit the North Fork image: somewhere between fruit bomb Sonoma examples and the less forthcoming products of Burgundy. By and large, Galluccio has created a friendly, supportive environment in which the winery can transition from its more mom-and-pop pre-Vince incarnation to the regional leader that its new owner wants it to be. However, quality remains a little uneven, and my own feeling is that Galluccio has mistakenly decided to focus too extensively on unproven varieties, like cabernet sauvignon, at the expense of less sexy—but more regionally appropriate—grapes. One thing's for sure: He's not going to sit back and be minor player, quietly easing his new baby into the next phase of its development. He has taken out huge ads in *Wine Spectator*, featuring himself, and has also donated considerably sums of money to the Cornell Cooperative Extension, a generally underfunded facility that nonetheless gallantly strives to do the agricultural research necessary to bring Long Island's wines up to par with other internationally prominent regions.

the lenz winery

631-734-6010; 800-974-9899

www.lenzwine.com

Eric Fry, Lenz's winemaker, is the polar opposite of a techno-vintner whose goal is to produce the most competent wine imaginable. Fry shuns that approach. His goal, basically, is to let it all hang out. That mojo suits him. A physically impressive man who sports a scraggly beard, long hair, and a mischie-vous twinkle in his eye—and whose favorite footwear, depending on the day's activity, is either sandals or work boots—Fry is capable of creating wines that will absolutely knock your socks off. He gets his hands dirty in the process; I've yet to see him without wine-stained fingers, even at posh events. Through Fry, the Lenz Winery has been able to announce itself as the North Fork's premier artisanal winery. They produce a wide variety of different wines, both reds and whites, but the guts of the operation are Fry's rich, highly extracted merlots. They put me in the mind of wines from the southern Rhône, so dense and brooding in good years. Of course, they can also tend toward the sludgy when the wine-maker's touch is off. But Fry is a sort of hippie mad scientist, and with a personality profile as vibrant as that, you take the good with the bad.

raphael

631-765-1100

www.raphaelwine.com

This stunning, faux Tuscan showplace toward the end of the Main Road is owned by John Petrocelli, Jr., who made his money in the construction business. His experience in the building trades is hard to miss inside this vast winery, with its heavy, soaring timbers, wrought-iron detailing, marble fire-places, and soaring rooftop cupola. Beneath the tasting room (and to call it a mere "room" scarcely does it justice), wine-maker Richard Olsen-Harbich works his alchemy in the North Fork's most technologically advanced winery. The passion here is for merlot and—a small amount of sauvignon blanc notwithstanding—nothing else. So serious are the Petrocelli's and Harbich about merlot that they have secured the services of M. Paul Pontailler, wine-maker at the legendary Bordeaux first-growth Château Margaux, as a consultant. Currently, the wines are still finding their legs, but that's to be expected as the estate's vineyards—and virtually all of Raphael's fruit is estate grown—mature. Plans here are to keep production limited to no more than 5,000 cases per year, thus ensuring quality. The range of wines is also streamlined, with then entry-level bottling starting at $15 and the top-of-the-line merlot coming in at $38. Given that some North Fork tasting rooms can get pretty cozy on a balmy Saturday in September, I've come to appreciate Raphael's indoor acreage, where you can really spread out. Two sights not to miss: the view of Harbich's jacketed stainless steel fermentation tanks, which can be viewed through a window that affords a glimpse of the cellar, and the massive, sloping crush pad that descends from the edge of the vineyards. A lot of engineering went into making this place the best, and my advice is to take some time to appreciate it.

schneider vineyards

❋ *2248 Roanoke Avenue*
Riverhead, NY
631-727-3334
www.schneidervineyards.com

For the first few years of its existence, this up-and-coming winery didn't actually have many physical holdings: no building, no vineyards, just grape contracts and some barrels that were kept as the Premium Wine Group, a custom-crush facility in Mattituck. Bruce Schneider and Christiane Baker-Schneider were definitely a new breed. Bruce, a marketing and PR professional, had parlayed a special MBA grant into startup capital for a wine business. From the beginning, he and his wife decided to take a slightly contrarian approach—the better to garner broad consumer attention. Rather than try to produce competitive merlot, for which the available grape supply was already pretty slim, they focused on

Cabernet Franc, an offbeat variety that was typically used to add aromatic complexity to merlot-cabernet blends. Lo and behold, they had hit on something. Advised by PWG's Russell Hearn, an Australian, they created a rich, extracted wine of reasonable complexity that captivated the palate of some wine critics. Then they took that good press and ran with it, nicknaming their flagship wine North Fork Franc and doing memorable stuff like having temporary tattoos of the slogan made up to pass out at events. For a while, they basically operated as négociants, a French tactic familiar to Burgundy lovers, in which the guy who sells the wine doesn't actually own the vineyards but instead contracts with reputable growers for fruit. However, success led to a modification of the business plan, and in June 2000, the Schneiders adopted the estate model, opening a winery to the public and developing their own vineyards. Their quality was already first rate, and this move should only enhance their reputation. At the moment, they produce both a value-priced red and white under their Potato Barn label, as well as a chardonnay and the aforementioned cab Franc, which remains one of the North Fork's best wines (bordering on the best, if you ask me.) Currently, their wines can be sampled at the Tasting Room in the town of Riverhead, which sits at the V between the North and South Forks. This is a temporary arrangement, however, as the Schneiders are now busy designing their own winery.

Although most of the action is up on the North Fork, the South Fork should not be neglected. This part of the state is better known for the Hamptons beach enclaves, which have long been where Manhattan's wealthy residents keep summer homes, but there are also three wineries, all of which produce excellent bottlings. The chief advantage to the South Fork is, of course, compactness. In my book, three wineries in one day is plenty. Then you can hit the beach in the afternoon.

wölffer estates

❊ *139 Sagg Road*
Sagaponack, NY
631-537-5106
www.wolffer.com

I'm a real Wölffer partisan, for two reasons. First, this is easily the most inviting and beautiful winery on all of Long Island, the new showplaces on the North Fork included. Owner Christian Wölffer, a charismatic international businessman, first ran his spread just outside Easthampton as a horse farm, and when he decided to make the move to wine-making, he brought a country gentleman's eye to the project. The result is an environment that radiates class. But I said there were two reasons, right? Reason number two is wine-maker Roman Roth, who I think is, across the board, the most skilled vintner in the region. I say this because Roth makes a wide variety of different wines, from a breezy bargain summer rosé that flies out of the tasting room to a robust Bordeaux-style red that sells for $100 and is produced in very limited quantities. You need chops to be able to cover that much ground and still keep your head screwed on straight. No problem for Roth, who's from Germany, but learned his wine-making in California and

Australia. (Heck, for a brief time Roth was also making cheese—the man's ambition knows no bounds.) The winery itself is a study in solidity, but not at the expense of an intimate quality. The Italianate main building, which houses the tasting room, winery, and cellars, is approached by steps that lead to a thick, oak door, bordered on either side by topiary evergreens. As tasting rooms go, Wölffer's is fairly conservative, but visitors who gather here will be surrounded by lovely paintings, no shortage of dark wood, and can study the vineyards that march right up to the rear terrace. Vineyard manager Richard Pisacano keeps his acreage healthy, neat, and productive, as the estate's considerable output of wines ranging from a steely Old World-style chardonnay to a plummy, easygoing merlot indicates. Wölffer's wines, especially their relatively high-acid chardonnay, also have more of a decent record for aging than their North Fork competition, perhaps attributable to the slightly warmer microclimate of the South Fork. I've come across chards from the early 1990s that reminded me of well-developed Chablis in their complexity and depth.

channing daughters

❊ *1927 Scuttlehole Road*
Bridgehampton, NY
631-537-7224
www.channingdaughters.com

If his neighbor Roman Roth is the most skilled wine-maker on Long Island, then Channing Daughters' Larry Perrine is the most underrated. Why? Pride, if you ask me. Perrine refuses to take anything other than the long view when it comes to wine. As far as he's concerned, his region is an evolving proposition, just beginning to come into its own; maturation shouldn't be rushed. Fortunately, Walter Channing—a wealthy businessman whose stark and fairly enormous sculptures, hewn from uprooted and inverted trees, cover the estate—has given Perrine plenty of room to maneuver. The result is a lineup of very serious, intelligently made wines that, in good vintages, really broadcast just how much potential the Long Island wine industry nurtures.

duck walk

❈ *231 Montauk Highway*
Water Mill, NY
631-726-7555
www.duckwalk.com

Duck Walk has been around for a while, but Dr. Herodotus Damianos' winery didn't pop onto a lot of people's radar until 2002, when it became embroiled in a lawsuit with a far better-known California winery. Dan Duckhorn, owner of Duckhorn Vineyards in Napa, decided that he could claim all rights to the word "Duck" in a winery's name. Damianos disagreed, forcing Duckhorn to take him to court. The outcome remains unsettled, but one thing's for sure: Duck Walk continues to produce a high-quality lineup of wines, from chardonnay to a cabernet sauvignon.

❈ the hudson valley

The Hudson Valley is visually spectacular, rising far, far above the wide and brooding Hudson River at points along its northerly progression. You can easily imagine the absolute awe that Henry Hudson and his band of explorers must have felt when they stumbled on this wild, immense waterway. These days, however, the Hudson Valley's wine industry is somewhat less than awe-inspiring; in fact, it's on a minor hiatus. But at one time, this was an extremely important American wine-making region, and vestiges of that glorious past are all around. In recent years, the Hudson Valley has become better known as a hotbed of artisanal farming (think heirloom hogs and rare vegetables), but there are still a few wineries worth checking out between trips to the unreconstructed hippie cheesemaker or the dot-com escapee and his flock of lambs. Beware: You'll probably encounter more out-of-fashion native varietal and French hybrids here than anywhere else in the state, but try to treat this as a learning experience. After all, given the preponderance of merlot and chardonnay everywhere else, how much longer will you be able to find an authentic taste of Baco Noir?

millbrook vineyards and winery

❋ *26 Wing Road*
Millbrook, NY
800-662-WINE
www.millbrookwine.com

Strangely, when people think of New York wine, they often think of Millbrook first—before anything from the North Fork, which has a buzzier media image, or the Finger Lakes, where the wines are superior. Millbrook has simply done a great job trading on its reputation as the best winery in New York state. But is that really true? Well, Millbrook is probably the best winery in the Hudson Valley. It's also set up best to receive tourists and day-tripppers from New York City. Lots happens at the Millbrook campus, where the barnlike main building rises from a sea of vineyards. Concerts, tours, special events—the whole nine yards. In fact, you could easily visit Millbrook, hang out for a while, taste some wine, then turn around and go home feeling as if you'd taken in all the Hudson Valley has to offer. You would be missing out, of course, but you'd enjoy some fine wines. Wine-maker John Graziano produces a decent little spread here, from the exotic Tocai Friulano, an unusual varietal that hails from Italy's northeast corner, to pinot noir and merlot. Nothing costs more than $30.

❋ the finger lakes

New York's secret weapon in the national wine wars. Sure, Long Island might have better PR and be a lot closer to New York City, but Finger Lakes is the only New York wine region that has successfully crafted a style of wine—Riesling—that can compete not just with California but with some impressive European examples. The country up here on the skinny glacial lakes that give the region its name is also utterly and completely beautiful (and sometimes rather fragrant, as it remains a very agricultural area). Most of the wineries are arranged along Seneca Lake, but a few can be found on nearby Cayuga Lake. This is about a five-hour drive north of New York City, but there are plenty of bed-and-breakfasts, not to mention the famous Watkins Glen race track, if that's your thing.

NOTE: General information about the Finger Lakes wine industry, as well as a (nearly) full listing of all wineries, can be found online at the Finger Lakes Wine Country Web site, www.fingerlakeswinecountry.com.

fox run vineyards

❋ *670 Route 14*
   Penn Yan, NY
   800-636-9786
   www.foxrunvineyards.com

Owner Scott Osborn cut his teeth in California before returning to Finger Lakes. He is probably the least provincial guy in a wine-making region that has, in the past, suffered from no shortage of provincialism. The man has a plan. His goal is to increase the supply of top-caliber grapes, by expanding vineyards plantings, especially in Riesling. He also hopes that Finger Lakes vintners can enhance their quality, boosting their best wines into a clearly premium category and better price per bottle, thus securing more capital to invest in marketing. If the Finger Lakes has a leader, Osborn is it. He also produces pretty good wine. Fox Run (and yes, there are foxes about) is one of the most technologically advanced and contemporary-looking of the new generation. I think their cabernet Franc is their best wine, but their pinot noir is coming along nicely, as are Riesling and chardonnay. The tasting room is an airy, open space where you can also obtain a delicious lunch, compliments of Fox Run's in-house café.

Blending: the winemaker's magic

Most wines are blended wines, meaning that although they may be labeled cabernet sauvignon, they contain a percentage of some other grape variety (just how much is dictated by law in important wine-making regions). The most highly prized wines in the world, the reds of the first-growth Chateaus of Bordeaux, are blended wines, made up of cabernet sauvignon, merlot, cabernet Franc, and in some cases Malbec and Petite Verdot. Australian winemakers commonly produce value-oriented wines that are blended from cabernet sauvignon and Shiraz. In France's southern Rhône Valley, Châteauneuf-du-Papes are assembled from as many as 13 different varieties. In fact, the only international wines that typically contain only one grape variety are pinot noir in Burgundy and California and cabernet sauvignon in the Napa Valley. Why do winemakers blend? To achieve consistent quality, for one thing, but also to produce a good wine in a year that might have seen poor performance from, say, cabernet sauvignon. Just add merlot to smooth things out!

lamoreaux landing wine cellars

❊ *9224 Route 414*
  Lodi, New York 14860
  607-582-6011
  www.lamoreauxwine.com

Easily the Finger Lakes' most architecturally dramatic winery, Lamoreaux merges elements of classic Upstate New York barn architecture with owner Mark Wagner's ideas about Greek temples. The result is an almost soaring Greek Revival structure that affords stunning views of Seneca Lake—but still functions as a working winery (barrels are stacked high rather than laid out, due to the cellar's small footprint). Wagner is a pinot noir enthusiast—many in the Finger Lakes are, citing their cooler growing climate—but Lamoreaux's portfolio of wines also includes chardonnay, Gewürztraminer, and sparkling wines.

red newt cellars & bistro

❊ *3675 Tichenor Road*
  Hector, NY 14841
  607-546-4100
  www.rednewt.com

Dave Whiting is the Finger Lakes best winemaker. It shows especially in his Rieslings, which can challenge Germany and Alsace for quality. With Standing Stone, Red Newt has thus far produced the only Finger Lakes whites that truly suggest strong aging potential. This is a result of two things: intelligent wine-making and grape sourcing; and local knowledge. Whiting knows his way around the region, having labored here for decades (he was briefly involved with Standing Stone, before the Macinskis went it alone). Red Newt's wine-making facility is no-nonsense, and the tasting room, while substantial, really plays second fiddle to the winery's bistro,

where Dave's wife, Debra, helms the stoves. The winery building itself is a modern affair, a simple, dark, wooden shape with
a decorative vineyard out front. From the deck, the views of
Seneca Lakes are extraordinary. A deeply pleasing place to
eat an early dinner and sample a taste or two of the Finger
Lakes' boundless future.

standing stone vineyards

❉ *9934 Route 414*
  Hector, NY
  800-803-7135
  www.standingstonewines.com

With Red Newt, a quality leader in the Finger Lakes region.
Owners Tom and Marti Macinski are, to put it mildly, winging
it (as much as you can wing it, having been in business since
1991). Their winery is a borderline shabby affair, a pale green
and yellow edifice that all but sinks into the landscape. Their
vineyards are full of weeds. But their Riesling and Gewürztraminer are out of this world. It just goes to show you that
talent and dedication can sometimes make up for a lack of
experience. What distinguishes the Macinskis from the competition is their commitment to getting their wines into the
Finger Lakes' nearest major market, New York City. Given the
generally very high quality of Finger Lakes whites, it's frankly
astonishing that they aren't better exposed in Manhattan.
Chalk it up to ingrained resistance. New Yorkers, if they're
even aware of the Finger Lakes at all, think of it as a sleepy
realm of farmers, not as a viable alternative to the Napa Valley. (It's worth pointing out that the "Flakes," as I like to call
them, have achieved a level of excellence with Riesling that
California can't hope to match—so it's not as if the Finger
Lakes ever has to think of itself as being in direct competition
with the Mondavis and Gallos.) As Tom and Marti develop

their brand, keep an eye out for their superb wines. Like New Zealand sauvignon blancs, their Gewürztraminer and Rieslings are bound to command higher prices in years to come.

the wine experience

Every other year, *Wine Spectator* magazine hosts its annual Wine Experience in New York. This is a long weekend of large-scale tastings, special seminars on food and wine conducted by the magazine's editors, and a gala ball with entertainment and, usually, a surprise or two (the mayor has been known to put in an appearance). How you spend depends on how much of a wine hootenanny you're interested in. The full monty costs more than a thousand bucks, But you can lay down just a bit more than a hundred for access to a Grand Tasting. The Grand Tastings are always great opportunities to check in on the world's finest wine producers; only those who have a wine that has scored more than 90 points ("Outstanding") on *Wine Spectator*'s 100-point scale are invited. What this usually means is a good chance to sample a superrare California "cult" cabernet, or an expensive French or Italian wine that you might otherwise only get a shot at if you sought it out on a restaurant wine list. The event is held in the fall and is advertised well in advance, both in issues of the magazine, and on the Web site, www.wine-spectator.com.

a brief glossary

Acidity: All wines are acidic to one degree or another. A skill-ful wine-maker balances acidity with tannin and fruitiness to create a harmonious composition. Too much acid throws the wine out of balance. But a wine with properly regulated acid-ity will have a refreshing aspect that, even in a robust vintage, brings a taster back for another sip.

Barrels: Usually made of oak. Coopers can, however, cus-tomize barrels extensively. Some wine-makers go so far as to travel to France and visit forests to pick out the trees that will eventually become their barrels. The main tool that the bar-relmaker has at his disposal is fire: The flavors that a barrel imparts to a wine can be greatly influenced by the degree of toast that is imparted by a skilled cooper. Toasting of barrels is very low-tech: Coopers light a fire and expose the interior for prescribed amounts of time, thereby producing a barrel with "light," "medium," or "heavy" toast. A barrel can be used only once, or many times, depending on what the wine-maker wants. One kind of wine that is neither fermented nor aged in oak is said in Australia to be "unwooded." In Amer-ica, they're sometimes said to be "unoaked."

Bouquet: An old-fashioned term that tries to define what an older wine smells like. Distinct from "nose" or "aroma," both of which address the way younger wines smell. In short, if you're talking bouquet, you're attempting to judge a wine that has some age to it.

Corked: The term for a wine tainted by TCA (2, 4, 6 trichloroanisole), a chemical compound that essentially destroys a wine's freshness. Corked wines smell musty and taste deflated. Some producers have sought to eliminate the problem—which some maintain afflicts one out of every 24 bottles—by moving to synthetic corks. Quite often, it's not the cork that's the problem, however—it's your wineglass, which can pick up all sorts of off aromas from soap or the cabinet it's stored in. It's a good idea to rinse your glasses, either with water or wine, before using them.

Cult wine: A California wine, generally a cabernet sauvignon–based bottling, produced in tiny quantities, often by a celebrity wine-maker, and sold at phenomenally high prices to an exclusive clientele. These wines are distributed almost solely by mailing lists, and the lists are profoundly difficult to get on. Big names are Colgin, Bryant Family, and Screaming Eagle. The wines themselves are rich, heavy, and dense. Critics maintain that they are all for show and will not age as well as the top Bordeaux they are meant to compete with.

Dry: The vast majority of wines produced worldwide are referred to as dry, meaning that most of their original sugar has been transformed into alcohol. Some important wines, however—notably German Riesling—do not have all their sugar fermented out. These wines are sometimes referred to as being off dry. The sugar that doesn't get fermented is called residual sugar.

Fermentation: The chemical process by which yeast transforms sugar into alcohol. All wines go through it. One of the by-products of fermentation is carbon dioxide. When champagne or sparkling wine is allowed to undergo a second fermentation in the bottle, this is what generates the bubbles.

First growth or prémier cru.: An important designation for Bordeaux. According to the famous Classification of 1855, revised in 1973, there are now five first-growth wineries in Bordeaux: Châteaux Lafite Rothschild, Mouton Rothschild, Latour, Haut-Brion, and Margaux.

Flight: In most cases, a grouping of wines that have something in common. For example, five Napa Valley chardonnay from the 1994 vintage, each from different producers. Typically, one encounters flights at professional tastings, wine courses, and wine bars. A flight can be more broadly defined, however, to mean simply a lineup of wines selected for tasting together. Not to be confused with vertical, which is a gathering of the same wine from different vintages.

Fruit bomb: Almost always a New World wine, high in alcohol, that strives to bowl you over with rich fruit flavor. Recently, wines that go for this flavor profile have fallen in for criticism for purists who think that the fruit-forward, New World style is erasing older, more subtle types of wine-making. Fruit bombs are sometimes derided—or lauded—as wines produced in the "international" style.

New World: The colloquial term for wines that aren't from Europe. The current New World consists of the United States, Australia, New Zealand, South America, and South Africa.

Oak: Often, but not always, wines spend some time in oak barrels before they're bottled. There are a variety of reasons for this. Sometimes, wine-makers want the oak to add depth and complexity to the wine. Other times, they just want the wine to pick up particular oak flavors, such as vanilla or toast. Less expensive wines will sometimes be dosed with oak chips or staves for a little extra flavor kick. But for wine-makers willing to spend the money, there are several types of barrels that predominate. French oak tends to be softer and less obtrusive. American oak is more aggressive, but popular because it can deliver a blast of charry flavor. Slovenian oak is something of a cult preoccupation, but it has adherents who see it as a third way, between pricey French and heavy-duty American oak.

Old World: The colloquial term for wines from Europe.

Quaffer, a.k.a. plonk,: an unsophisticated wine meant to go down easy. Nothing fancy, a chug-a-lug wine.

Quality-to-Price Ratio (QPR): Merely a way of expressing, in a slightly highfalutin way, whether a wine is a good buy or not. If a wine scores 97 points on the 100-point scale, and it costs $20, it has an excellent QPR.

Super Tuscan: A recent wine category, invented in Italy in the past 20 years. Essentially, it means a Tuscan wine produced in a more fruit-forward, New World style, usually with cabernet sauvignon or merlot included in the blend.

Tannin: A component in red wines that comes mainly from skins and seeds during maceration, a period before fermentation from grape juice into wine. Tannin makes your cheeks feel prickly and often indicates that a wine has aging potential (wine critics will sometimes commend a tannic wine for its "structure"). Of course, when tannin is totally out of balance with the fruit in a wine, it can mean that the wine was crudely made. A heavily tannic wine isn't much fun to drink, as it does what it's supposed to: turn your tongue to leather.

Variety/Varietal: Grapes come in varieties; wines come in varietal. When merlot is a grape, it's a variety. When it's a bottled wine, it's a varietal. Easy as that.

Vertical: A lineup of wines, all from the same producer (say, Château Lafite Rothschild, a first-growth Bordeaux), covering several vintage years. You might start with 1990 and work your way up to 2000. The idea is to get a sense of how vintage affects a wine.

the new york book of wine

Z

index by neighborhood

acknowledgments

I owe a considerable debt of thanks to the numerous people who put me in a position to write this book, and also those who helped execute it. Thanks first of all to my agent, Dan Mandel, and my editor at Rizzoli/Universe, Kathleen Jayes, who supported and encouraged me from the start. Rizzoli/Universe's Holly Rothman expertly guided the book through the publishing process. I would never have had the chance to start writing about wine without the support of Russ Smith and Andrey Slivka at *New York Press*. All my colleagues at *Wine Spectator* and her sister publication, *Cigar Aficionado*, provided what amounted to a graduate degree in a life with wine. I am especially grateful to Thomas Matthews, Per-Henrik Mansson, Gordon Mott, Daniel Sogg, Jack Bettridge, and David Savona. Most important, I must thank Maria Russo, my companion and confidant in all things; my in-laws, Mario and Jacqueline Russo, for their warmth and generosity; and my one-of-a-kind mother, Nora DeBord, for her endless kindness and affirmation.

Matthew DeBord

Matthew DeBord is a former editor at *Wine Spectator*. He has written for many publications, including *The New York Observer*, *Salon*, and *Food & Wine*. A graduate of Clemson and New York universities, he lives in Brooklyn with his wife and daughter.